Classic
POTATO DISHES

Classic POTATO DISHES

Sue Ashworth • Carol Handslip • Jane Hartshorn
Kathryn Hawkins • Wendy Lee • Cara Hobday • Louise Steele
Rosemary Wadey • Pamela Westland

P

· PARRAGON ·

First published in Great Britain in 1996 by
Parragon
Unit 13–17
Avonbridge Trading Estate
Atlantic Road
Avonmouth
Bristol BS11 9QD

Published in paperback 1997

ISBN: 0-7524-1613-2 (hardback)
ISBN: 0-7525-2340-6 (paperback)

Printed in Italy

Produced by Haldane Mason, London

Acknowledgements
Editor: Lisa Dyer
Design: Digital Artworks Partnership Ltd
Photography: Karl Adamson, Sue Atkinson, Iain Bagwell, Martin Brigdale,
Amanda Heywood, Joff Lee, Patrick McLeavey and Clive Streeter
Home Economists: Sue Ashworth, Carole Handslip, Jane Hartshorn, Kathryn Hawkins,
Cara Hobday, Wendy Lee, Louise Steele, Rosemary Wadey, Pamela Westland

Material in this book has previously appeared in *Balti Cooking, Barbecues,
Caribbean Cooking, Cooking For One & Two, Cooking On A Budget,
Indian Side Dishes, Indian Vegetarian Cooking, Italian Regional Cooking,
Low-fat Cooking, Mexican, Microwave Meals, Pasta Cooking, Picnics, Pizza,
Quick & Easy Indian Cooking, Quick & Easy Meals, Recipes with Yogurt,
Sensational Salads, Soups & Broths, Vegetarian Barbecues* and *Vegetarian Main Meals*

Note
Cup measurements in this book are for American cups.
Tablespoons are assumed to be 15ml. Unless otherwise stated, milk is assumed to be
full-fat, eggs are standard size 2 and pepper is freshly ground black pepper.

CONTENTS

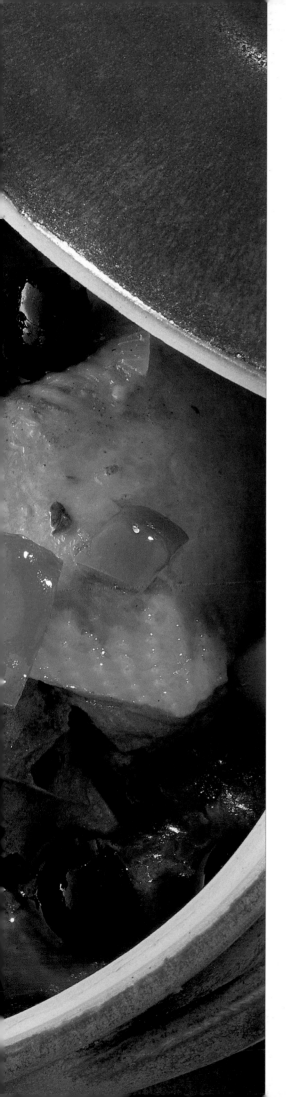

INTRODUCTION

One of the best qualities of the potato is that it tastes delicious with many other ingredients, spices and herbs, happily marrying flavours to produce dishes with entirely different characteristics. As a result, many cuisines contain dozens of potato recipes – in French cookery, for example, you would find literally hundreds of potato dishes. On the following pages you will find some of the best French recipes, along with a diverse selection from countries around the world. You will also find recipes suitable for all occasions, from soups, salads, snacks, light meals and side dishes, through to main meals, pies and bakes. Classic favourites, such as Potatoes Lyonnaise, are featured, along with some inspired new creations, such as filled tortillas, pasties and samosas.

Potatoes are such an integral part of everyday cooking in Europe that it is hard to imagine they had to be introduced at all! The potato is, in fact, a native plant of Ecuador, where it was discovered by the invading Spaniards around 1550. It was known as the *batata* or *battato*, and it is thought that early English settlers in America traded with the Spaniards for it, though it was not until Sir Walter Raleigh's expedition of 1584 that the potato was brought to Great Britain. At that time, it was regarded as a delicacy, and it was two hundred years before potatoes were developed commercially, at the end of the 18th century.

The nutritional benefits of the potato are highly regarded. With today's emphasis on healthy eating, the potato has come into its own as a natural, wholesome food. Essentially a complex carbohydrate or 'starchy' food, potatoes supply our bodies with an important source of energy. Starchy foods are now rightly regarded as an essential element of a healthy, well-balanced diet, and they should form a high proportion of our food intake. Not only do potatoes supply us with energy, they are also a useful source of vitamins and fibre too. All potatoes supply fibre, especially in the skins, and potatoes also contain vitamin C and B6, along with niacin, riboflavin, thiamin, and such minerals as copper, iron, magnesium, potassium, phosphorus and zinc. Sweet potatoes are also very nutritious, containing vitamin A, calcium, iron, niacin and potassium.

All aspects of potato cuisine are covered in this comprehensive cook book. If you are looking for a potato recipe to accompany a special meal, or if you just want inspiration for some tasty snacks, then you will find what you are looking for within these pages. The simple, step-by-step instructions will guide you through each recipe, so whether you are a culinary whiz in the kitchen or a novice cook, the results will be every bit as tasty!

SELECTING AND STORING POTATOES

The best rule for new-season potatoes is to buy them in small quantities when you need them and use them within a day or two of purchase to enjoy their flavour at its best. Any soil sticking to the skin that is damp is a sure sign of freshness, and the skins should rub away easily. Discard any potatoes that are showing a tendency to turn green – this is caused by exposure to light, and these potatoes should not be eaten. Main-crop potatoes should be free from damage, dirt and growth shoots. Avoid any potatoes with green discolouration. Choose those in good shape and buy in bulk if you have sufficient storage space available. For small amounts of potatoes, keep them in a vegetable rack in a cool, dark place. If you have bought them in a polythene bag, empty them out, as the moisture that may form within the bag can cause the potatoes to rot. Brown paper bags are ideal for storage.

Remember to handle potatoes carefully, as they can bruise easily, especially sweet potatoes. Keep in mind that warmth causes potatoes to sprout, damp makes them rot, and light turns potatoes green; so a cool, dry, dark place that is free from frost is the ideal spot. If you have bought a sack of main-crop potatoes, keep it raised from the ground to allow air to circulate. Avoid keeping any potatoes close to strong-smelling foods, such as onions, which could taint their flavour.

If properly stored, new potatoes or thin-skinned boiling potatoes will keep for about two weeks, with baking or sweet potatoes keeping for up to six months. Cooked potatoes will keep for up to three days in the refrigerator, while cooked sweet potatoes will keep for up to a week. Mashed or puréed cooked potatoes can be frozen for two or three months, but do not freeze raw potatoes as they loose their firmness and texture.

THE PICK OF THE CROP

You may think that all potatoes will do the same job, and to some extent you would be right, but you wouldn't be getting the best from them! Different varieties have their own characteristics, and each is suited to a particular use. Thankfully, you don't have to become acquainted with all the many different potato varieties to know which purpose they are best suited to – in greengrocer shops and supermarkets, you will find some guidance on the potatoes' labelling and packaging to show the best way to use that specific variety. The package should indicate if a potato is suited to baking, mashing, roasting or for making French fries. However, if the potatoes are sold loose, then you will need to ask the greengrocer or the supermarket manager for guidance.

The colourful names of potato varieties are increasingly referred to, meaning that you can quickly identify a potato for a particular purpose. Ask for the potatoes by these names when you buy them; a discerning customer that knows the varieties will be well respected in any shop!

Each type of potato can have different varieties of texture, from floury or mealy to creamy or waxy, meaning that they lend themselves to different treatments. Usually floury potatoes, which describes the texture after cooking, means it is a baking potato, and a waxy potato will signify a boiling potato. You will find some that are good all-rounders, suitable for many purposes, though you may like to try a wide range to pinpoint your preferences. The size of potatoes can vary enormously, from tiny ones weighing less than 15 g/π oz to huge ones weighing in at 500 g/1 lb or more. Here is a round-up of some of the more popular varieties:

Alcmaria This variety is suitable for all-round use, though especially good in salads.

Arran Pilot As these potatoes keep their shape well, they are excellent in potato salads.

Belle de Fontenay With a pale yellow skin and yellow flesh, these potatoes are excellent when boiled or steamed and served in salads or stews.

Blue The blue varieties, such as Blue Carib and All Blue, are American and they have a greyish blue skin and a blue flesh. They have a subtle flavour that is best enjoyed when simply boiled.

Cara This is a large, round main-crop potato, suitable for all uses, though especially good for baking.

Catriona A yellow-skinned variety with cream-coloured flesh, it has a delicious flavour and a floury texture. Steam, bake or roast this type.

Desirée A good, all-round variety with red skin and pale yellow flesh.

Estima Another all-purpose variety, this attractive potato has pale yellow skin and flesh, and an even, oval shape.

Epicure This variety has white-fleshed skin with a pink tinge and a creamy flesh that has very good flavour. It is excellent in salads, but also good for boiling and mashing.

Finnish Yellow Waxed A yellow-fleshed America variety which is great for potato salads or boiled in the skin.

German Fingerling A small, light-skinned American potato with a yellow flesh. It is best simply boiled.

Idaho Also called Russet potatoes, which includes such varieties as Russet Burbank and Butte. This favourite from America is a baking potato with reddish brown skin. It is known as an Idaho even though it is produced in other US states.

King Edward A favourite main-crop variety with creamy-coloured flesh, suitable for all-round use.

Maris Bard This is an early potato variety with good cooking qualities. It has white skin and flesh.

Maris Piper A very popular main-crop potato with a white skin and creamy-coloured flesh. This is an excellent all-rounder, especially good for boiling, mashing, baking and roasting.

Pentland Dell A popular main-crop potato with a long oval shape and creamy white flesh with a white skin. It is suitable for French fries, baking, mashing and roasting.

Pentland Javelin A widely grown potato, with excellent cooking qualities and a very white skin and flesh. Look out for it after the first early potatoes have appeared.

Pentland Squire A perfect choice for baking or mashing, because of its floury texture. This is a white-skinned, white-fleshed variety, although it can occasionally have a russet appearance.

Pink Fir Apple This main-crop potato has the characteristics of new potatoes. It has excellent flavour and is particularly good in salads. It is a long, slightly knobbly potato with a pink flesh and it has a firm, waxy texture.

Red Pontiac An American variety with a dry, floury texture. It is often sold as new or boiling potatoes and is best when boiled.

Romano This red-skinned variety has a creamy flesh and is a popular main-crop choice.

Rose Fir A small, waxy potato from America with a pink to red skin and a creamy consistency. It is best boiled.

White Rose A long, white, waxy variety from America, suitable for boiling, but may also be baked or made into French fries.

Wilja A good basic variety with all-round use. It has a yellow skin with a netted appearance and a pale yellow flesh. It is very useful for boiling and steaming, and for using in salads and casseroles, as it keeps its shape during cooking.

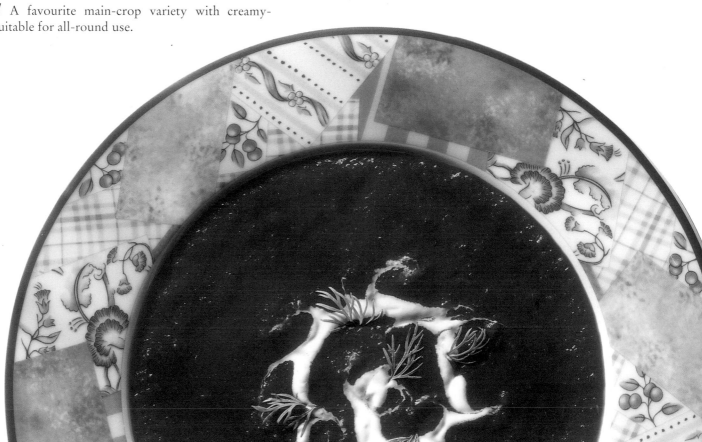

PREPARING AND COOKING POTATOES

Cut out eyes, sprouts or any discoloured areas. Use a potato peeler or proper peeling knife to peel potatoes, so that you can peel them thinly. Thick peeling is wasteful, as many of the nutrients are contained close to the skin. You will need to rinse the potatoes well after peeling and pat them dry with kitchen paper or a clean tea towel. You can make French fries with unpeeled potatoes, which is a good way to conserve more nutrients; just scrub the potatoes very thoroughly, in the same way as you would prepare new potatoes.

To boil potatoes, cut them into even-sized pieces so they all cook evenly at the same time, put them into cold water in a saucepan, add a little salt if you wish, and bring to the boil. Then cover, reduce the heat and simmer gently until the potatoes are tender. Serve immediately to prevent the potatoes from breaking up. Potatoes that are kept hot for a long period of time will lose more nutrients. Mashed potatoes make a warm, comforting dish in the winter months. Just mash boiled potatoes with a fork or potato masher, then add butter and milk and beat until light and fluffy with a wooden spoon or hand-held electric beater. Season with salt, pepper and a little freshly ground nutmeg, if you like.

Baked potatoes are the simplest to prepare. Choose large, even-sized potatoes, free from blemishes. Scrub them well, cut out any damaged or discoloured areas or eyes and prick several times with a fork. Place the potatoes on a baking sheet and bake at 220°C/425°F/Gas Mark 7 for 1–1½ hours until soft.

You can bake them in a microwave oven if you prefer, although they won't have the same crispy skin. One large potato will take about 8 minutes. Remember to prick the skin first and turn the potato once halfway through the cooking time. Times will vary according to the size of potato and the number you are cooking.

For roast potatoes, cut peeled potatoes into even-sized pieces. Parboil them for 10 minutes to reduce the roasting time, or just roast them from raw if you prefer. To cook them, place the potatoes in a large roasting pan with some hot fat and bake at 230°C/450°F/Gas Mark 8 for 40 minutes to an hour before removing. You may like to coat the potatoes in flour before adding them to the hot fat. Larger roast potatoes will absorb less fat, and will therefore have a slightly lower calorie content. This applies to French fries – large, straight-cut potatoes will absorb less fat, and have less calories, than smaller, crinkle-cut ones.

Here are some simple ways to add interest to your plain mashed, boiled or baked potatoes.

- Try adding a drizzle of good-quality extra-virgin olive oil instead of butter to mashed potatoes. Alternatively, sauté a couple of crushed garlic cloves in the olive oil before adding to the mash.

- Sun-dried tomatoes in olive oil, drained and chopped, give mash an Italian slant. You may like to add some chopped fresh oregano or basil too.

- Sauté a small onion in butter until golden, stir it through mash with plenty of ground black pepper and some Parmesan cheese. Pile the mash into a serving dish, top with grated Cheddar cheese and grill until bubbling

- Mix canned tuna fish that has been drained and flaked with chopped onion, sweetcorn and chopped red or green (bell) pepper. Dress it with a little olive oil and vinegar and use to top baked potatoes.

- Combine chopped roast chicken, chopped spring onion (scallion) and mayonnaise to taste. Use to top baked potatoes.

- Combine chopped cooked chicken or turkey with mayonnaise, flavour it with mild curry powder, and use to top baked potatoes.

- Combine soft cheese with grated Cheddar, a little chopped spring onion (scallion) and some snipped chives. Use to top baked potatoes.

- Mix cooked peeled prawns (shrimp) in a couple of tablespoons of commercially prepared seafood sauce and use to top baked potatoes.

- Sauté snipped bacon, chopped onion and red (bell) pepper in butter, and use to top baked potatoes.

- Mix chopped cooked ham with cottage cheese and pineapple. Use to top baked potatoes.

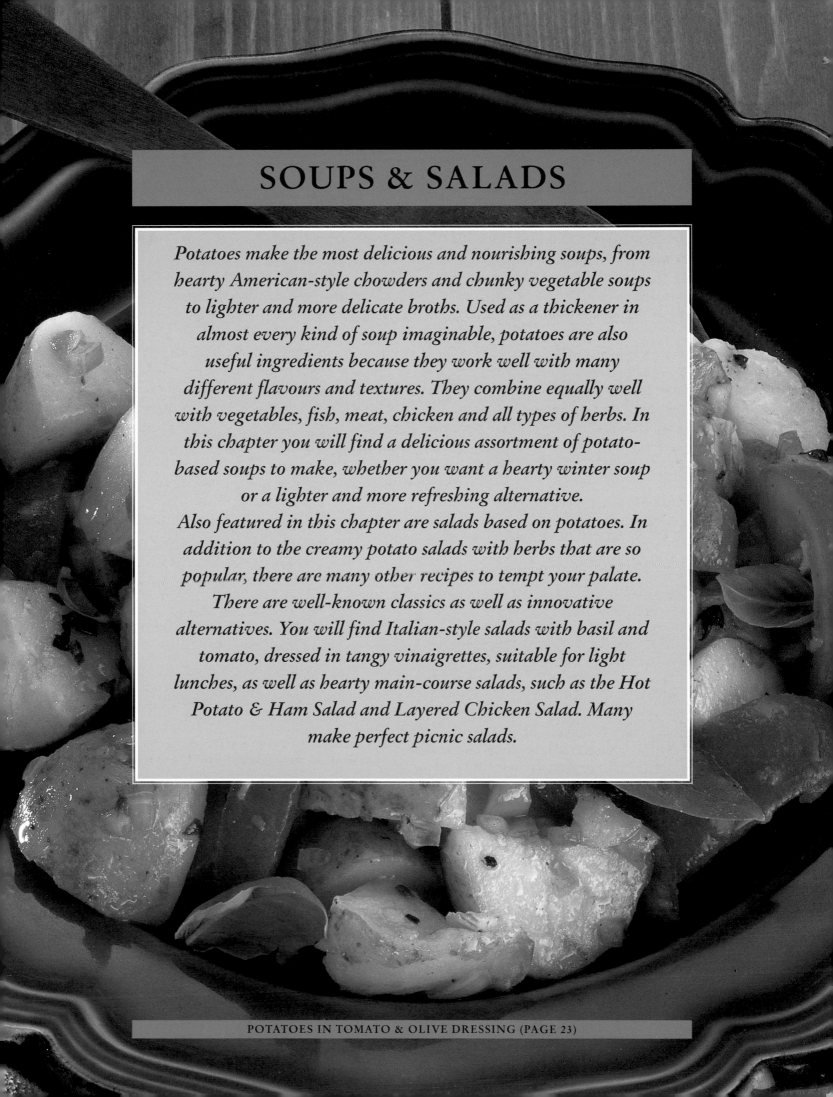

SOUPS & SALADS

Potatoes make the most delicious and nourishing soups, from hearty American-style chowders and chunky vegetable soups to lighter and more delicate broths. Used as a thickener in almost every kind of soup imaginable, potatoes are also useful ingredients because they work well with many different flavours and textures. They combine equally well with vegetables, fish, meat, chicken and all types of herbs. In this chapter you will find a delicious assortment of potato-based soups to make, whether you want a hearty winter soup or a lighter and more refreshing alternative.

Also featured in this chapter are salads based on potatoes. In addition to the creamy potato salads with herbs that are so popular, there are many other recipes to tempt your palate. There are well-known classics as well as innovative alternatives. You will find Italian-style salads with basil and tomato, dressed in tangy vinaigrettes, suitable for light lunches, as well as hearty main-course salads, such as the Hot Potato & Ham Salad and Layered Chicken Salad. Many make perfect picnic salads.

POTATOES IN TOMATO & OLIVE DRESSING (PAGE 23)

FISH & SEAFOOD CHOWDER

Served with warm crusty bread and a salad, this tasty soup makes a substantial lunch or supper dish.

SERVES 4

INGREDIENTS:
1 kg/2 lb mussels in their shells
1 large onion, thinly sliced
2 garlic cloves, chopped
3 bay leaves
few sprigs fresh parsley
few sprigs fresh thyme
300 ml/½ pint/1¼ cups water
250 g/8 oz smoked haddock fillets
500 g/1 lb potatoes, peeled and diced
4 celery sticks, thickly sliced
250 g/8 oz can sweetcorn, drained and rinsed
150 ml/¼ pint/⅔ cup natural yogurt
1 tsp cornflour (cornstarch)
150 ml/¼ pint/⅔ cup dry white wine or dry cider
¼ tsp chilli powder, or to taste
pepper
2 tbsp chopped fresh parsley

1 ▼ Scrub the mussels, pull off the 'beards' and rinse in several changes of cold water. Discard any open shells that remain open when tapped.

2 Put the onion, garlic, bay leaves, parsley and thyme in a large saucepan and pour on the water. Add the mussels, cover and cook over a high heat for 5 minutes, shaking the pan once or twice.

3 ▼ Line a colander with muslin (cheesecloth) and stand it in a bowl. Strain the mussel liquor into the bowl. Remove and shell the mussels and set them aside. Discard the vegetables and herbs and reserve the liquor.

4 ▲ Put the haddock, potatoes and celery into the rinsed saucepan, add

600 ml/1 pint/2½ cups of cold water and bring to the boil. Cover the pan and simmer for 10 minutes. Remove the haddock with a fish slice and skin, bone and flake it. Remove the vegetables with a slotted spoon and strain the liquor into the reserved seafood liquor.

5 Return the cooking liquor to the rinsed saucepan, add the sweetcorn and bring to the boil. Stir together the yogurt and cornflour (cornstarch) to make a smooth paste. Stir in a little of the fish liquor, then pour it into the pan. Stir until the yogurt is well blended, then add the reserved mussels, haddock, potatoes and celery.

6 Add the white wine, season with chilli powder and pepper and heat the soup gently, without boiling. Taste and adjust the seasoning if necessary.

7 Transfer to a warm serving dish and sprinkle with the chopped parsley. Serve hot.

SMOKED FISH CHOWDER

A really substantial soup with a subtle smoky flavour and thick with vegetables and fish.

SERVES 4

INGREDIENTS:

90 g/3 oz streaky bacon, chopped
500 g/1 lb potatoes, diced finely
600 ml/1 pint/2½ cups milk
1 fresh bay leaf
about 425 g/14 oz can sweetcorn, drained
350 g/12 oz thin fillet smoked haddock or cod, skinned
4 spring onions (scallions), white and green parts sliced thinly
salt and pepper
crusty bread, to serve

1 ▼ Fry the bacon in a saucepan for 2 minutes, then add the potatoes, milk, bay leaf and seasoning. Bring to the boil and simmer for 5 minutes.

2 ▼ Add the sweetcorn, fish and spring onions (scallions) and cook for a further 5 minutes.

3 Use 2 forks to break the fish into large flakes.

4 ▼ Turn the soup into a large soup tureen or individual bowls and serve with chunks of crusty bread.

SAGE & ONION CHOWDER

This thick, creamy onion soup, with plenty of fragrant fresh sage, is full of chopped bacon, potatoes and sweetcorn.

SERVES 4–6

INGREDIENTS:
60 g/2 oz/¼ cup butter or margarine
4 onions, sliced very thinly or chopped
1–2 garlic cloves, crushed
4 slices lean bacon, chopped
2 tbsp plain (all-purpose) flour
900 ml/1½ pints/3½ cups chicken or
  vegetable stock
500 g/1 lb potatoes, diced very finely
300 ml/½ pint/⅓ cup creamy milk
about 200 g/7 oz can sweetcorn, well
  drained
1 tbsp chopped fresh sage, or 1½ tsp
  dried sage
2 tbsp white wine vinegar
salt and pepper
sprigs of fresh sage, to garnish
warmed bread, to serve

1 ▼ Melt the butter or margarine in a large saucepan and fry the onions and garlic very gently for about 15 minutes until soft but not coloured.

2 Add the chopped bacon and continue to fry for a few minutes, allowing the onions to colour a little. Stir in the flour and cook for a further minute or so.

3 ▼ Add the stock and bring to the boil. Then add the potatoes and seasoning and simmer gently for 20 minutes.

4 ▼ Add the milk and sweetcorn and bring back to the boil, then add the sage and vinegar and simmer for a further 10–15 minutes until the potatoes are very tender but not broken up.

5 Adjust the seasoning, garnish with sprigs of sage and serve while hot with warmed bread.

LEEK, POTATO & CARROT SOUP

A quick chunky soup, ideal for a snack or a quick lunch. The leftovers can be puréed to make one portion of creamed soup for the next day.

SERVES 2

INGREDIENTS:
*1 leek, about 175 g/6 oz
1 tbsp oil
1 garlic clove, crushed
750 ml/1¼ pints/3 cups chicken or
    vegetable stock
1 bay leaf
¼ tsp ground cumin
175 g/6 oz/1 cup potatoes, diced
125 g/4 oz/1 cup carrot, grated
    coarsely
salt and pepper
chopped fresh parsley, to garnish*

PUREED SOUP:
*5–6 tbsp milk
1–2 tbsp double (heavy) cream, crème
    fraîche or soured cream*

1 ▼ Trim off some of the coarse green part of the leek, then slice thinly and rinse in cold water. Drain well.

2 Heat the oil in a saucepan, add the leek and garlic, and fry gently for 2–3 minutes until soft but barely coloured. Add the stock, bay leaf, cumin and seasoning, and bring to the boil.

3 Add the diced potato to the saucepan, cover and simmer gently for 10–15 minutes until the potato is just tender but not broken up.

4 ▼ Add the grated carrot and simmer for a further 2–3 minutes. Adjust the seasoning, discard the bay leaf and serve sprinkled liberally with chopped fresh parsley.

5 ▲ To make a puréed soup, first blend the leftovers (about half the original soup) in a blender or food processor, or press through a sieve (strainer), until smooth and then return to a clean saucepan with the milk. Bring to the boil and simmer for 2–3 minutes. Adjust the seasoning and stir in the cream before serving sprinkled with the parsley.

SMOKY HADDOCK SOUP

Smoked haddock gives this soup a good rich flavour, while mashed potatoes and cream thicken and enrich the stock.

SERVES 4–6

INGREDIENTS:
250 g/8 oz smoked haddock fillet
1 onion, chopped finely
1 garlic clove, crushed
600 ml/1 pint/2½ cups water
600 ml/1 pint/2½ cups milk
250–350 g/8–12 oz/1–1½ cups hot
  mashed potatoes
30 g/1 oz/2 tbsp butter
about 1 tbsp lemon juice
6 tbsp double (heavy) cream, soured
  cream or natural fromage frais
4 tbsp chopped fresh parsley
salt and pepper

1 Put the fish, onion, garlic and water into a saucepan. Bring to the boil, cover and simmer gently for about 15–20 minutes until the fish is tender.

2 ▼ Remove the fish from the pan; strip off the skin and remove all the bones. Flake the flesh finely.

3 Return the skin and bones to the cooking liquor and simmer for 10 minutes. Strain, discarding the skin and bones, and pour the liquor into a clean saucepan.

4 Add the milk, flaked fish and seasoning to the saucepan, bring to the boil and simmer for about 3 minutes.

5 ▲ Gradually whisk in sufficient mashed potato to give a fairly thick soup, then stir in the butter and sharpen the soup to taste with a little lemon juice.

6 ▼ Add the cream, soured cream or fromage frais and 3 tablespoons of the parsley. Reheat gently, sprinkle with the remaining parsley and serve.

VICHYSSOISE

This is a classic creamy soup made from potatoes and leeks. To achieve the delicate pale colour, be sure to use only the white parts of the leeks. Vichyssoise is also excellent served hot.

SERVES 4–6

INGREDIENTS:
3 large leeks
45 g/1½ oz/3 tbsp butter or margarine
1 onion, sliced thinly
500 g/1 lb potatoes, chopped
900 ml/1½ pints/3¾ cups chicken or vegetable stock
2 tsp lemon juice
pinch of ground nutmeg
¼ tsp ground coriander
1 dried bay leaf
1 egg yolk
150 ml/¼ pint/⅔ cup single (light) cream
salt and white pepper
snipped fresh chives or crisply fried and crumbled bacon, to garnish

1 ▲ Trim the leeks and remove most of the green part (it can be served as a vegetable). Slice the white part of the leeks very finely.

2 Melt the butter or margarine in a saucepan and fry the leeks and onion gently for about 5 minutes without browning, stirring from time to time.

3 ▼ Add the potatoes, stock, lemon juice, seasoning, nutmeg, coriander and bay leaf to the pan and bring to the boil. Cover and simmer for about 30 minutes until all the vegetables are very soft.

4 Cool the soup a little, discard the bay leaf and then press the soup through a sieve (strainer), or blend in a food processor or blender, until smooth. Pour into a clean saucepan.

5 ▼ Blend the egg yolk into the single (light) cream, add a little of the soup to the mixture and then whisk it all back into the soup and reheat gently without boiling. Adjust seasoning to taste.

6 Leave to cool, and then cover and chill thoroughly in the refrigerator. Garnish the soup with snipped chives or crisply fried and crumbled bacon and serve chilled.

MICROWAVE BEETROOT SOUP

A deep red soup of puréed beetroots and potatoes, this makes a stunning first course. Adding a swirl of soured cream and a few sprigs of dill gives a very pretty effect.

SERVES 4

INGREDIENTS:
1 onion, chopped
350 g/12 oz potatoes, diced
1 small cooking apple, peeled, cored and grated
3 tbsp water
1 tsp cumin seeds
500 g/1 lb cooked beetroot, peeled and diced
1 dried bay leaf
pinch of dried thyme
1 tsp lemon juice
600 ml/1 pint/2½ cups hot vegetable stock
4 tbsp soured cream
salt and pepper
sprigs of fresh dill, to garnish

1 Place the onion, potatoes, apple and water in a large bowl. Cover and cook on high power for 10 minutes.

2 ▲ Stir in the cumin seeds and cook on high power for 1 minute.

3 ▲ Stir in the beetroot, bay leaf, thyme, lemon juice and stock. Cover and cook on high power for 12 minutes, stirring halfway through.

4 Leave to stand, uncovered, for 5 minutes. Remove the bay leaf. Strain the vegetables and reserve the liquid. Blend the vegetables with a little of the reserved liquid in a food processor or blender, until smooth and creamy. Alternatively, mash the ingredients or press the soup through a sieve (strainer).

5 Pour the vegetable purée into a clean bowl with the reserved liquid and mix well. Season to taste. Cover and cook on high power for 4–5 minutes until piping hot.

6 ▲ Serve the soup in warmed bowls. Swirl 1 tablespoon of soured cream into each serving and garnish with a few sprigs of fresh dill.

MINTED PEA & YOGURT SOUP

This deliciously refreshing soup is also nutritious. It is extremely tasty when served chilled – in which case you may like to thin the consistency a little more with extra stock, yogurt or milk, as wished.

SERVES 6

INGREDIENTS:
2 tbsp vegetable oil or ghee
2 onions, peeled and coarsely chopped
250 g/8 oz potato, peeled and coarsely
   chopped
2 garlic cloves, peeled
2.5 cm/1 inch piece ginger root, peeled
   and chopped
1 tsp ground coriander
1 tsp ground cumin
1 tbsp plain (all-purpose) flour
900 ml/1½ pints/3¾ cups vegetable stock
500 g/1 lb frozen peas
2-3 tbsp chopped fresh mint, to taste
salt and pepper
150 ml/¼ pint/⅔ cup strained thick
   yogurt
½ tsp cornflour (cornstarch)
300 ml/½ pint/1¼ cups milk
a little extra yogurt, to serve
   (optional)
sprigs of fresh mint, to garnish

1 ▼ Heat the oil or ghee in a saucepan, add the onions and potato and cook gently for 3 minutes. Stir in the garlic, ginger, coriander, cumin and flour and cook for 1 minute, stirring.

2 Add the stock, peas and half the mint and bring to the boil, stirring.

3 Reduce the heat, cover and simmer gently for 15 minutes or until the vegetables are tender.

4 ▼ Blend the soup, in batches, in a blender or food processor to a purée. Return the mixture to the pan and season to taste. Blend the yogurt with the cornflour (cornstarch) and stir into the soup.

5 ▼ Add the milk and bring almost to the boil, stirring all the time. Cook very gently for 2 minutes. Serve hot, with a swirl of extra yogurt, if wished, and garnished with the mint.

INDIAN BEAN SOUP

This soup is substantial enough to serve as a main meal with wholemeal (whole wheat) bread. Black-eye beans (peas) are used here, but red kidney beans or chick-peas (garbanzo beans) may be added if preferred.

SERVES 4–6

INGREDIENTS:

4 tbsp vegetable oil or ghee
2 onions, peeled and chopped
250 g/8 oz/1½ cups potato, peeled and cut into chunks
250 g/8 oz/1½ cups parsnip, peeled and cut into chunks
250 g/8 oz/1½ cups turnip or swede (rutabaga), peeled and cut into chunks
2 celery sticks, trimmed and sliced
2 courgettes (zucchini), trimmed and sliced
1 green (bell) pepper, cored, deseeded and cut into 1 cm/½ inch pieces
2 garlic cloves, crushed
2 tsp ground coriander
1 tbsp paprika
1 tbsp mild curry paste
1.25 litres/2 pints/5 cups vegetable stock
salt
475 g/15 oz can black-eye beans (peas), drained and rinsed
chopped fresh coriander (cilantro), to garnish (optional)

1 Heat the oil or ghee in a saucepan, add all the prepared vegetables, except the courgettes (zucchini) and (bell) pepper, and cook over a medium heat for 5 minutes, stirring frequently. Add the garlic, coriander, paprika and curry paste and cook for 1 minute, stirring.

2 ▼ Stir in the stock and season with salt to taste. Bring to the boil, cover and simmer gently for 25 minutes, stirring occasionally.

3 ▼ Stir in the beans (peas), sliced courgettes (zucchini) and green (bell)

pepper, cover and continue cooking for a further 15 minutes or until all the vegetables are tender.

4 ▲ Blend 300 ml/½ pint/1¼ cups of the soup mixture (about 2 ladlefuls) to a purée in a food processor or blender. Return the mixture to the soup in the saucepan and reheat until piping hot.

5 Sprinkle with chopped coriander (cilantro), if using and serve hot.

MINESTRONE WITH PESTO

This is one of the many versions of minestrone, which always includes vegetables, pasta and rice, and often beans. This soup is flavoured with pesto, so often added to pasta dishes.

SERVES 6

INGREDIENTS:
*175 g/6 oz/scant 1 cup dried cannellini
    beans, soaked overnight
2.5 litres/4 pints/10 cups water or stock
1 large onion, peeled and chopped
1 leek, trimmed and thinly sliced
2 celery sticks, very thinly sliced
2 carrots, peeled and chopped
3 tbsp olive oil
2 tomatoes, skinned and roughly
    chopped
1 courgette (zucchini), trimmed and
    thinly sliced
2 potatoes, peeled and diced
90 g/3 oz elbow macaroni (or other
    small macaroni)
salt and pepper
4–6 tbsp grated Parmesan*

PESTO:
*2 tbsp pine kernels (nuts)
5 tbsp olive oil
2 bunches fresh basil, stems removed
4–6 garlic cloves, crushed
90 g /3 oz/¾ cup Pecorino or Parmesan,
    grated
salt and pepper*

1 ▼ Drain the beans, rinse and place in a saucepan with the measured water or stock. Bring to the boil, cover and simmer gently for 1 hour.

2 ▲ Add the onion, leek, celery, carrots and oil. Cover and simmer for 4–5 minutes.

3 Add the tomatoes, courgette (zucchini), potatoes, macaroni and seasoning. Cover again and continue to simmer for about 30 minutes or until very tender.

4 Meanwhile, make the pesto. Fry the pine kernels (nuts) in 1 tablespoon of the oil until pale brown, then drain.

5 Put the basil into a food processor or blender with the nuts and garlic. Process until well chopped. Gradually add the oil, bit by bit, until smooth. Turn the sauce into a bowl, add the cheese and seasoning and mix thoroughly.

6 ▲ Stir 1½ tablespoons of the pesto into the soup until well blended, simmer for a further 5 minutes and adjust the seasoning. Serve very hot, sprinkled with the cheese.

HUNGARIAN SAUSAGE SOUP

A rich, warming soup, based on the famous Hungarian goulash, which uses beef instead of sausage.

SERVES 4

INGREDIENTS:
2 tbsp olive oil
2 onions, chopped
2 garlic cloves, chopped
1 tbsp paprika
500 g/1 lb potatoes, diced
1 red (bell) pepper, deseeded and diced
425 g /14 oz can chopped tomatoes
1 tbsp tomato purée (paste)
1 fresh bay leaf
2 tsp caraway seeds
900 ml/1½ pints/3¾ cups beef stock
175 g/6 oz kabanos sausage, sliced
2 tbsp chopped fresh parsley
4 tbsp soured cream
salt and pepper
crusty bread, to serve

1 ▼ Heat the oil in a saucepan and fry the onion over a high heat for 2 minutes. Add the garlic and paprika and fry briefly.

2 ▼ Add the potato, red (bell) pepper, tomatoes, tomato purée (paste), bay leaf, caraway seeds, stock and seasoning.

3 Cover and simmer for 10–15 minutes, then add the kabanos and parsley and cook for a further 2 minutes.

4 ▲ Pour the soup into warm bowls and spoon a little of soured cream into each bowl. Serve with crusty bread.

POTATOES IN TOMATO & OLIVE DRESSING

The warm potatoes quickly absorb the wonderful flavours of olives, tomatoes and olive oil. This salad is delicious when served warm, but it is also good served cold.

SERVES 4

INGREDIENTS:
*750 g/1½ lb waxy potatoes
1 shallot
2 tomatoes
1 tbsp chopped fresh basil
salt*

TOMATO AND OLIVE DRESSING:
*1 tomato, skinned and chopped finely
4 black olives, pitted and chopped
   finely
4 tbsp olive oil
1 tbsp wine vinegar
1 garlic clove, crushed
salt and pepper*

1 Cook the potatoes in boiling salted water for 15 minutes until tender.

2 ▼ Drain the potatoes well, chop roughly and put into a bowl. Chop the shallot. Cut the tomatoes into wedges and add the shallot and tomatoes to the warm potatoes.

3 ▼ To make the dressing, put all the ingredients into a screw-top jar and mix together thoroughly.

4 ▲ Pour the dressing over the potato mixture and toss thoroughly. Transfer the salad to a serving dish and sprinkle with the chopped fresh basil.

MEXICAN SALAD

Cooked new potatoes and blanched cauliflower are combined with carrots, olives, capers and gherkins in a tangy mustard dressing for a salad that is suitable as an accompaniment or as a main dish.

SERVES 4

INGREDIENTS:

500 g/1 lb small new potatoes, scraped
salt
250 g/8 oz small cauliflower florets
1–2 carrots, peeled
3 large gherkins
2–3 spring onions (scallions), trimmed
1–2 tbsp capers
12 pitted black olives
1 iceberg lettuce or other lettuce leaves

DRESSING:

1½–2 tsp Dijon mustard
1 tsp sugar
2 tbsp olive oil
4 tbsp thick mayonnaise
1 tbsp wine vinegar
salt and pepper

TO GARNISH:

1 ripe avocado
1 tbsp lime or lemon juice

1 Cook the potatoes in salted water until they are just tender; drain, cool and either dice or slice. Cook the cauliflower in boiling salted water for 2 minutes. Drain, rinse in cold water and drain again.

2 Cut the carrots into narrow julienne strips and mix with the potatoes and cauliflower.

3 ▼ Cut the gherkins and spring onions (scallions), slicing on the diagonal, and add them to the salad together with the capers and black olives.

4 ▲ Arrange the lettuce leaves on a large serving plate or bowl or in individual bowls and spoon the salad over the lettuce.

5 ▲ To make the dressing, whisk all the ingredients together until completely emulsified. Drizzle the dressing over the salad.

6 ▼ Cut the avocado into quarters, then remove the stone (pit) and peel. Cut into slices and dip immediately in the lime or lemon juice. Use to garnish the salad just before serving.

GARDEN SALAD

This chunky salad includes tiny new potatoes tossed in a minty dressing, and has a mustard dip for dunking.

SERVES 6–8

INGREDIENTS:
500 g/1 lb tiny new or salad potatoes
4 tbsp French salad dressing or
*   vinaigrette*
2 tbsp chopped fresh mint
225 g/8 oz broccoli florets
125 g/4 oz sugar snap peas or
*   mangetout (snow peas), trimmed*
2 large carrots
4 celery sticks
1 yellow or orange (bell) pepper,
*   halved, cored and deseeded*
1 bunch spring onions (scallions),
*   trimmed (optional)*
1 head chicory (endive)

MUSTARD DIP:
6 tbsp soured cream
3 tbsp thick mayonnaise
2 tsp balsamic vinegar
1¼ tsp coarse-grain mustard
½ tsp creamed horseradish
good pinch of brown sugar
salt and pepper

1 Cook the potatoes in boiling salted water until just tender – about 10 minutes. While they cook, combine the dressing or vinaigrette and mint.

2 ▼ Drain the potatoes thoroughly, add to the dressing while hot, toss well and leave until cold, giving an occasional stir.

3 ▼ To make the dip, combine the soured cream, mayonnaise, vinegar, mustard, horseradish, sugar and seasoning. Transfer to a serving bowl, cover and refrigerate until ready to serve.

4 Cut the broccoli into bite-sized florets and blanch for 2 minutes in boiling water. Drain and toss immediately in cold water; when cold, drain thoroughly.

5 Blanch the sugar snap peas or mangetout (snow peas) in the same way but only for 1 minute. Drain, rinse in cold water and drain again.

6 Cut the carrots and celery into sticks about 6 × 1 cm/2½ × ½ inches; and slice the (bell) pepper or cut into cubes. Cut off some of the green part of the spring onions (scallions), if using, and separate the chicory (endive) leaves.

7 ▲ Arrange the vegetables attractively in a fairly shallow bowl with the potatoes piled up in the centre. Serve accompanied with the mustard dip.

POTATO & SMOKED HAM MAYONNAISE

This delicious mixture of potato, egg and smoked ham, mixed with a mustard mayonnaise, is ideal for a light lunch. You can use sliced frankfurters cut into cubes instead of the smoked ham if you prefer.

SERVES 4

INGREDIENTS:
750 g/1½ lb new potatoes, scrubbed
4 spring onions (scallions), chopped
2 tbsp French dressing or vinaigrette
150 ml/¼ pint/⅔ cup mayonnaise
3 tbsp thick natural yogurt
1 tbsp Dijon mustard
2 eggs
250 g/8 oz slice of smoked ham
3 gherkins
2 tbsp chopped fresh dill

1 Cook the potatoes in boiling salted water for 15 minutes until just tender, then drain.

2 ▼ Cut into pieces and put into a bowl while still warm with the spring onion (scallion) and dressing and mix together well.

3 Mix the mayonnaise, yogurt and mustard together. Set aside.

4 Boil the eggs for 12 minutes, then plunge into cold water to cool. Shell and chop roughly.

5 ▼ Cut the smoked ham into cubes and slice the gherkins.

6 ▲ Add the cubed ham and sliced gherkins to the potatoes with the chopped egg. Pour over the mayonnaise and mustard mixture and mix the salad together carefully to combine.

7 Transfer the potato salad to a large serving dish, sprinkle with the chopped fresh dill and serve.

THREE-WAY POTATO SALAD

There's nothing to beat the flavour of new potatoes, served just warm in a delicious dressing.

EACH DRESSING SERVES 4

INGREDIENTS:
500 g/1 lb new potatoes for each dressing
fresh herbs, to garnish

LIGHT CURRY DRESSING:
1 tbsp vegetable oil
1 tbsp medium curry paste
1 small onion, chopped
1 tbsp mango chutney, chopped
6 tbsp natural yogurt
3 tbsp single (light) cream
2 tbsp mayonnaise
salt and pepper
1 tbsp single (light) cream, to garnish

WARM VINAIGRETTE DRESSING:
6 tbsp hazelnut oil
3 tbsp cider vinegar
1 tsp coarse-grain mustard
1 tsp caster (superfine) sugar
few fresh basil leaves, torn into shreds
salt and pepper

PARSLEY, SPRING ONION (SCALLION) & SOURED CREAM DRESSING:
150 ml/¼ pint/⅔ cup soured cream
3 tbsp light mayonnaise
4 spring onions (scallions), trimmed and chopped finely
1 tbsp chopped fresh parsley
salt and pepper

1 To make the Light Curry Dressing, heat the vegetable oil in a saucepan and add the curry paste and onion. Fry together, stirring frequently, for about 5 minutes until the onion is soft. Remove from the heat and leave to cool slightly.

2 ▼ Mix together the mango chutney, yogurt, cream and mayonnaise. Add the curry mixture and blend together. Season with salt and pepper.

3 ▼ To make the Warm Vinaigrette Dressing, whisk the hazelnut oil, cider vinegar, mustard, sugar and basil together in a small jug or bowl. Season with salt and pepper.

4 ▲ To make the Parsley, Spring Onion (Scallion) & Soured Cream Dressing, mix all the ingredients together until thoroughly combined. Season with salt and pepper.

5 Cook the potatoes in lightly salted boiling water until just tender. Drain well and leave to cool for 5 minutes, then add the chosen dressing, tossing to coat. Garnish with fresh herbs, and spoon a little single (light) cream on to the potatoes if you have used the curry dressing, and serve.

HOT POTATO & HAM SALAD

This is a very adaptable salad. With potatoes as a base, you can vary the additional ingredients, using egg, pickled herring or beetroot in place of the smoked ham. It is excellent served as a light lunch.

SERVES 4

INGREDIENTS:
175 g/6 oz smoked ham
500 g /1 lb salad potatoes
6 spring onions (scallions), white and
    green parts sliced
3 gherkins, sliced
4 tbsp mayonnaise
4 tbsp thick natural yogurt
2 tbsp chopped fresh dill
salt

1 ▼ Cut the ham into 3.5 cm/1½ inch long strips.

2 ▼ Cut the potatoes into 1 cm /½ inch cubes and cook in boiling salted water for 8 minutes until tender.

3 ▲ Drain the potatoes and return to the saucepan with the spring onions (scallions), ham and cucumber.

4 ▼ Mix in the mayonnaise, yogurt and dill and stir to coat the potatoes. Transfer to a warmed dish and serve.

BASIL, POTATO & PIMENTO SALAD

Bags of mixed salad leaves, available from supermarkets, can be used instead of the lettuces in this robust and colourful salad. The vinaigrette is added to warm potatoes so they absorb some of the flavour.

SERVES 4

INGREDIENTS:
750 g/1½ lb new potatoes, scrubbed
¼ tsp salt
1 lollo rosso or oak leaf lettuce
½ cos (romaine) lettuce
watercress or rocket (arugula) leaves
1 small red onion, sliced finely
125 g/4 oz canned red pimento, drained
12 pitted black olives
handful of fresh basil leaves
salt and pepper

VINAIGRETTE:
6 tbsp olive oil
3 tbsp red wine vinegar
1 tsp Dijon mustard
pinch of caster (superfine) sugar
salt and pepper

1 ▼ Put the potatoes into a saucepan of cold water. Bring to the boil, add the salt, then cover and simmer for about 20 minutes until tender.

2 ▼ Meanwhile make the vinaigrette by whisking the olive oil, vinegar, mustard, sugar and seasoning together in a small bowl.

3 Drain the potatoes, cut into quarters and place in a large bowl. Pour over the vinaigrette and leave to cool.

4 Arrange the lettuce leaves, watercress or rocket (arugula) and

onion on 4 serving plates. Pile one quarter of the dressed potatoes on each salad. Alternatively arrange the ingredients on a large serving platter.

5 ▲ Slice the pimentos into narrow strips and arrange over the potatoes. Place 3 olives on each serving. Tear the basil leaves into shreds and sprinkle over the salads. Season with extra salt and pepper and serve.

LAYERED CHICKEN SALAD

This layered main course salad has lively tastes and textures. For an interesting variation, substitute canned tuna for the chicken. You can also use a commercial vinaigrette or Caesar salad dressing instead of this homemade dressing.

SERVES 4

INGREDIENTS:
750 g/1½ lb new potatoes, scrubbed
1 red (bell) pepper, halved, cored and
　deseeded
1 green (bell) pepper, halved, cored and
　deseeded
2 small courgettes (zucchini), sliced
1 small onion, thinly sliced
3 tomatoes, sliced
350 g/12 oz cooked chicken, sliced
snipped fresh chives, to garnish

YOGURT DRESSING:
150 g/5 oz/⅔ cup natural yogurt
3 tbsp mayonnaise
1 tbsp snipped fresh chives
salt and pepper

1 Put the potatoes into a large saucepan of cold water. Bring to the boil, then reduce the heat. Cover and simmer for 15–20 minutes until tender.

2 Meanwhile place the (bell) pepper halves, cut side down, under a preheated hot grill (broiler) and grill (broil) until the skins blacken and begin to char. Remove and cover with a clean, damp cloth. Leave to cool, then peel off the skins and slice the flesh. Set aside.

3 ▼ Cook the courgettes (zucchini) in a small amount of lightly salted boiling water for 3 minutes. Rinse with cold water to cool quickly and set aside.

4 ▼ Make the dressing. Mix the yogurt, mayonnaise and snipped chives together in a small bowl. Season well with salt and pepper.

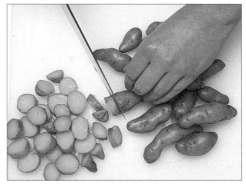

5 ▲ Drain, cool and slice the potatoes. Add them to the dressing and mix well to coat evenly. Divide between 4 serving plates. Top each plate with one quarter of the (bell) pepper slices and cooked courgettes (zucchini). Layer one quarter of the onion and tomato slices, then the sliced chicken, on top of each serving. Garnish with snipped chives and serve.

BACON & EGG SALAD WITH CRISPY FRIED POTATOES

Crispy bacon bits, hard-boiled (hard-cooked) egg and cubes of crispy fried potato make a very tasty salad on a bed of lettuce. Four standard eggs can be substituted for the quail's eggs.

SERVES 4

INGREDIENTS:
250 g/8 oz potatoes, scrubbed
¼ tsp salt
3 tbsp olive oil
15 g/½ oz/1 tbsp butter
125 g/4 oz smoked bacon
8–12 quail's eggs, hard-boiled
   (hard-cooked)
1 large bag mixed lettuce leaves

LEMON DRESSING:
3 tbsp olive oil
1 tsp finely grated lemon rind
1½ tbsp lemon juice
1 tbsp chopped fresh parsley or
   coriander (cilantro)
salt and pepper

1 Put the potatoes into a large saucepan of cold water. Bring to the boil, add the salt and then reduce the heat. Cover and simmer for 15 minutes until just tender. Cool, peel and dice.

2 ▼ Heat the olive oil and butter in a large frying pan (skillet). Add the diced potatoes and gently fry over a medium–high heat for 8–10 minutes until browned and crisp. When crispy, remove with a perforated spoon and drain on paper towels.

3 ▼ Meanwhile grill (broil) the bacon under a preheated hot grill (broiler) until very crisp. Drain on paper towels and snip into tiny pieces. Halve the cooked quail's eggs.

4 Rinse the lettuce and arrange on 4 plates. Scatter one quarter of the potatoes over each salad. Divide the eggs between the plates and sprinkle each salad with crispy bacon bits.

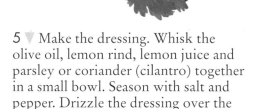

5 ▼ Make the dressing. Whisk the olive oil, lemon rind, lemon juice and parsley or coriander (cilantro) together in a small bowl. Season with salt and pepper. Drizzle the dressing over the salads and serve.

RUSSIAN SALAD

This classic salad is perfect for the winter months, as it makes the most of a selection of root vegetables. For a lighter dressing, substitute a low-fat mayonnaise or else mix equal quantities of low-fat natural yogurt with salad cream or mayonnaise.

SERVES 4

INGREDIENTS:
3 medium potatoes, peeled and
    quartered
½ tsp salt
1 carrot
1 turnip
½ small cauliflower, broken into tiny
    florets
60 g/2 oz/½ cup frozen peas, thawed
2 tomatoes, skinned, deseeded and
    diced
60 g/2 oz/½ cup cooked peeled prawns
    (shrimp)
60 g/2 oz/½ cup cooked ham, diced

CAPER DRESSING:
4 gherkins, chopped
1 tbsp capers
4–5 tbsp salad cream or mayonnaise
salt and pepper

TO SERVE:
¼ iceberg lettuce, shredded
1 cooked beetroot, diced
gherkins
stuffed green olives, sliced
sprigs of fresh parsley

1 Put the potatoes into a large saucepan of cold water. Bring to the boil, add the salt, then reduce the heat. Cover and simmer for 15–20 minutes until tender. Drain, cool slightly and dice. Set aside.

2 ▼ While the potatoes are cooking, dice the carrot and turnip and cook with the cauliflower in lightly salted boiling water for 5–8 minutes until tender. Drain and leave to cool.

3 ▼ In a large bowl, mix together the potatoes, carrot, turnip, cauliflower, thawed peas and tomatoes. Add the

prawns (shrimp) and diced ham and stir well to combine.

4 ▼ Make the dressing. Combine the gherkins and capers with the salad cream or mayonnaise in a small bowl. Season with salt and pepper. Add to the salad and stir well to coat evenly.

5 Arrange the lettuce on 4 serving plates. Pile one quarter of the salad mixture on each plate. Arrange little mounds of beetroot at the side of each salad. Using a sharp knife, make several lengthways cuts in each gherkin, leaving one end intact and then fanning out the gherkin. Garnish the salads with the gherkin fans, sliced olives and parsley.

SNACKS & LIGHT MEALS

*This chapter celebrates the versatility of potatoes, showing
you how to create a fabulous array of hors-d'oeuvres and
party nibbles as well as quick and healthy lunches or snacks.
Along with such favourites as potato skins with dips and
filled jacket potatoes, which are suitable for family lunches
and for children, there are more elegant dishes, such as Crab
& Potato Balls and Almond Potato Bites, that would be ideal
to serve as starters for more sophisticated dinner parties.
A wide selection of potato fritters and cakes is also featured,
from spicy and exotically flavoured recipes to milder cheese
and herb varieties. There are samosas, pasties and other little
deep-fried pastry parcels that are filled with a blend of
ingredients; some of which are vegetarian while others
include meat. For those who like the combination of eggs
and potatoes, there are several omelette dishes, such as the
frittata-style Spanish Omelette and the colourful Flamenco
Eggs. There are also Picnic Omelette Squares which are
delicious served cold, like tapas.*

DEVILLED NEW POTATOES

This is a way of giving potatoes, or any other root vegetable you have to hand, the star treatment. A barbecue needs smaller things like this to keep your diners happy while they wait for the main event. You will need to soak the cocktail sticks (toothpicks) in hand-hot water for 20 minutes before using.

SERVES 6–8

INGREDIENTS:
20 cocktail sticks (toothpicks)
500 g/1 lb baby new potatoes
olive oil for brushing
10 slices streaky bacon
20 small sage leaves

1 ▼ Bring a pan of water to the boil and add the potatoes. Boil for 10 minutes, then drain.

2 ▼ Brush the potatoes all over with olive oil.

3 ▼ Cut each bacon slice in half widthways. Holding each piece at one end, smooth and stretch it with the back of a knife.

4 ▲ Wrap a piece of bacon around each potato enclosing a sage leaf and securing with a cocktail stick (toothpick).

5 Cook over a hot barbecue (grill), or under a preheated hot grill (broiler), for 6–7 minutes, turning occasionally. Serve hot or cold.

CRAB & POTATO BALLS

These make an unusual first course. They are very popular in the Dominican Republic, where they may also be made with chopped prawns (shrimp). Serve them with a rich tomato sauce, if you like.

MAKES 30

INGREDIENTS:
500 g/1 lb potatoes, cut into chunks
45 g/1½ oz/3 tbsp butter
2 egg yolks
60 g/2 oz/½ cup Edam cheese, grated
1 tbsp finely chopped fresh flat-leaf
  parsley
1 onion, finely chopped
500 g/1 lb/2 cups crab meat, shredded
plain (all-purpose) flour, for coating
1 egg, beaten
60 g/2 oz/½ cup dry white breadcrumbs
vegetable oil, for deep-frying
salt and pepper

TO GARNISH:
lemon or lime wedges
spinach leaves

1 ▼ Cook the potatoes in boiling salted water until tender. Drain and mash with 30 g/1 oz/2 tablespoons of the butter, the egg yolks, cheese, parsley and seasoning. Set aside.

2 Heat the remaining butter in a small frying pan (skillet) and gently fry the onion until soft but not brown.

3 Transfer the onion to a bowl and leave to cool.

4 ▼ Add the crab meat and mashed potato to the onion and combine well. Form into 30 small equal-sized balls. Place on a baking sheet lined with baking parchment and refrigerate for at least 30 minutes.

5 Put the flour and breadcrumbs in separate shallow dishes or on plates. Roll the balls in the flour, dip them in the beaten egg and then coat evenly with the breadcrumbs.

6 ▼ Half fill a deep-fat fryer or saucepan with oil and heat to 190°C/375°F, or until a cube of bread browns in 40 seconds. Deep fry the balls in batches for 5–6 minutes until golden brown all over. Remove with a perforated spoon and drain on paper towels. Keep warm until all the balls have been cooked.

7 Serve garnished with lemon or lime wedges and spinach leaves.

PAKORAS

These vegetable fritters are simple to make and extremely good to eat. They may be served as a tasty starter or as an accompaniment to a main course.

SERVES 4–6

INGREDIENTS:
125g/4 oz broccoli
1 onion
2 potatoes
175 g/6 oz/1½ cups gram flour
1 tsp garam masala
1½ tsp salt
½ tsp chilli powder
1 tsp cumin seeds
200 ml/7 fl oz/just under 1 cup water
vegetable oil, for deep-frying
sprigs of coriander (cilantro), to garnish

1 ▽ Cut the broccoli into small florets, discarding most of the stalk and cook in a pan of boiling, salted water for 4 minutes. Drain well, return to the pan and shake dry over a low heat for a few moments. Place the broccoli on absorbent paper towels to completely dry while preparing the other vegetables.

2 Peel and thinly slice the onion and separate into rings. Peel and thinly slice the potatoes and pat dry.

3 ▽ Place the gram flour in a bowl with the garam masala, salt, chilli powder and cumin seeds. Make a well in the centre, add the water and mix to form a smooth batter. Dip the vegetables into the batter to coat them thoroughly.

4 ▲ One-third fill a deep-fat fryer or pan with oil and heat to 190°C/375°F, or until a cube of bread browns in 30 seconds. Lower the vegetables into the hot oil and fry, in batches, for 3–4 minutes or until golden brown and crisp. Drain on absorbent paper towels and keep warm while cooking the remainder in the same way. Serve the pakoras hot, garnished with coriander (cilantro).

SAMOSAS WITH SPICY DIP

A spicy filling of minced (ground) meat and vegetables is enclosed in a pastry crescent and is excellent served with a dip. If you are packing the samosas for a picnic, or in a lunch-box, fry the samosas 2–3 hours in advance.

MAKES 16

INGREDIENTS:

1 onion, finely chopped
1 garlic clove, crushed
1 tsp freshly grated ginger root
2 tbsp oil
1 carrot, grated coarsely
1½ tsp garam masala
125 g/4 oz/⅓ cup cooked minced (ground) beef, pork or ham
125 g/4 oz/⅔ cup cooked peas
175 g/6 oz/1 cup cooked potatoes, diced finely
salt and pepper

PASTRY:

250 g/8 oz/2 cups plain (all-purpose) flour
¼ tsp salt
30 g/1 oz/2 tbsp butter or margarine
about 100 ml/3½ fl oz/scant ½ cup cold water
vegetable oil, for deep-frying

SPICY DIP:

150 ml/¼ pint/⅔ cup thick mayonnaise
3 tbsp soured cream or fromage frais
1½ tsp curry powder
¼ tsp ground coriander
1 tsp tomato purée (paste)
2 tbsp mango chutney, chopped
1 tbsp chopped fresh parsley

1 To make the filling, fry the onion, garlic and ginger root in the oil until soft. Add the carrot and fry for 2–3 minutes. Stir in the garam masala and 4 tablespoons water, season, and simmer gently until almost all the liquid is absorbed. Remove the pan from the heat, stir in the meat, peas and potatoes and leave the mixture to cool.

2 To make the pastry, sift the flour and salt into a bowl and rub in (cut in) the butter. Add sufficient of the water to mix to a smooth, elastic dough, kneading continually. Cut the dough into 16 pieces and keep covered. Dip each piece into a little oil, or coat lightly with flour, and roll out to a 12 cm/5 inch circle.

3 ▼ Put 1–2 tablespoons of the filling on one side of each pastry circle, dampen the edge, fold over and seal firmly. Keep the samosas covered with a damp cloth.

4 ▼ In a deep-fat fryer or pan, heat the oil to 180–190°C/350–375°F, or until a cube of bread browns in about 30 seconds. Fry the samosas a few at a time for 3–4 minutes until golden brown, turning once or twice. Drain on paper towels.

5 To make the dip, combine all the ingredients in a separate bowl. Serve the samosas hot or cold with the dip.

VEGETABLE & CASHEW SAMOSAS

These nutty little fried pastries are really quite simple to make. Serve them hot as a starter to an Indian meal or cold as a tasty picnic or lunch-box snack.

MAKES 12

INGREDIENTS:
350 g/12 oz potatoes, peeled and diced
salt
125 g/4 oz frozen peas
45 ml/3 tbsp vegetable oil
1 onion, peeled and chopped
2.5 cm/1 inch piece ginger root, peeled and chopped
1 garlic clove, peeled and crushed
1 tsp garam masala
2 tsp mild curry paste
½ tsp cumin seeds
2 tsp lemon juice
60 g/2 oz/½ cup unsalted cashews, coarsely chopped
vegetable oil, for shallow frying
sprigs of coriander (cilantro), to garnish
mango chutney, to serve

PASTRY:
250 g/8 oz/2 cups plain (all-purpose) flour
60 g/2 oz/¼ cup butter
75 ml/6 tbsp/⅓ cup warm milk

1 Cook the potatoes in a saucepan of boiling, salted water for 5 minutes. Add the peas and cook for a further 4 minutes or until the potato is tender. Drain well. Heat the oil in a frying pan, add the onion, potato and pea mixture, ginger, garlic and spices and fry for 2 minutes. Stir in the lemon juice and cook gently, uncovered, for 2 minutes. Remove from the heat, slightly mash the potato and peas, then add the cashews, mix well and season with salt.

2 ▲ To make the pastry, put the flour in a bowl and rub in (cut in) the butter. Mix in the milk to form a dough. Knead lightly and divide into 6 balls. Roll out each ball on a lightly floured surface to an 18 cm/7 inch round. Cut each in half.

3 ▼ Divide the filling equally between each semi-circle of pastry, spreading it

out to within 5 mm/¼ inch of the edges. Brush the edges of pastry all the way round with water and fold over to form triangular shapes, sealing the edges well together to enclose the filling completely.

4 ▲ One-third fill a large, deep-fat fryer or pan with oil and heat to 180°C/ 350°F, or until a cube of bread browns in 30 seconds. Fry the samosas, a few at a time, turning frequently until golden brown and heated through. Drain on paper towels and keep warm while cooking the remainder in the same way. Garnish with coriander (cilantro) sprigs and serve hot.

TUNA & VEGETARIAN PARCELS

I first encountered this recipe in a Fijian–Indian restaurant in Sydney. In order to quell our hunger as we waited for our food, we were served these memorable tuna parcels. Each filling recipe makes enough to fill all the pastry.

MAKES 32

INGREDIENTS:
PASTRY:
500 g/1 lb/4 cups plain (all-purpose) flour
¼ tsp turmeric
¼ tsp salt
100 g/3¼ oz/scant ½ cup ghee or clarified butter
about 200 ml/7 fl oz/scant 1 cup milk, mixed with a little lemon juice

TUNA FILLING:
¼ tsp ground turmeric
¼ tsp chilli powder
1 tsp ground cumin
1 tsp ground coriander
200 g/7 oz can tuna, drained
60 g/2 oz/½ cup frozen peas, cooked
60 g/2 oz/½ cup boiled potatoes, diced
salt and pepper

VEGETARIAN FILLING:
250 g/8 oz white potatoes, boiled
425 g/14 oz can artichoke hearts, drained and blended to a purée
1 tsp black pepper, ground
2 tsp coriander seeds, ground
1 tsp cumin seeds, ground
¼ tsp fenugreek seeds, ground
2 large tomatoes, skinned, deseeded and chopped
90g /3 oz/½ cup frozen peas, cooked

SAUCE:
6 anchovies
2 tbsp natural yogurt

1 To make the pastry, sift the flour, turmeric and salt into a bowl. Rub in (cut in) the ghee or butter. Add enough milk to form a fairly soft dough. Cover and set aside.

2 To make the tuna filling, roast the spices in a large frying pan (skillet). Remove from the heat and add the tuna, peas and potatoes. Stir well and season. Use to fill the pastry.

3 ▼ To make the vegetarian filling, mash the potatoes and combine with the artichokes. Roast the spices in a large frying pan (skillet). Remove from the heat and add the potato mixture. Stir well to combine. Carefully fold in the tomatoes and peas. Season and use to fill the pastry.

4 ▼ Roll out the pastry and cut out 16 12 cm/5 inch circles. Cut each circle in half and put a teaspoonful of the tuna or vegetarian filling on each half.

5 Brush the edges with milk and fold each half over to form a triangle. Seal well, and crimp the edges. Bake in a preheated oven at 190°C/375°F/ Gas Mark 5.

6 To make the sauce, mash the anchovies, mix with the yogurt and season. Serve with the hot parcels.

POTATO SKINS WITH GUACAMOLE DIP

Although avocados do contain fat, if they are used in small quantities with the right balance of ingredients, you can still enjoy their creamy texture.

SERVES 4

INGREDIENTS:
4 250 g/8 oz baking potatoes
2 tsp olive oil
coarse sea salt and pepper
snipped fresh chives, to garnish

GUACAMOLE DIP:
175 g/6 oz ripe avocado
1 tbsp lemon juice
2 ripe, firm tomatoes, chopped finely
1 tsp grated lemon rind
100 g/3¼ oz/½ cup medium-fat soft cheese with herbs and garlic
4 spring onions (scallions), chopped finely
few drops of Tabasco sauce
salt and pepper

1 Bake the potatoes directly on the oven shelf in a preheated oven at 200°C/400°F/Gas Mark 6 for 1¼ hours until tender. Remove from the oven and allow to cool for 30 minutes. Reset the oven to 220°C/425°F/Gas Mark 7.

2 ▼ Halve the potatoes lengthways and scoop out 2 tablespoons of the flesh from the middle of each potato. Slice in half again. Place the potato skins on a baking sheet and brush the flesh side lightly with oil. Sprinkle with salt and pepper.

3 Bake for a further 25 minutes until the potato skins are golden and crisp.

4 ▲ Meanwhile make the guacamole dip. Halve the avocado and discard the stone (pit). Peel off the skin and mash the flesh with the lemon juice in a small bowl.

5 ▼ Transfer to a large bowl and mix with the remaining ingredients. Cover and chill until required.

6 Drain the potato skins on paper towels and transfer to a warmed serving platter. Garnish with chives. Serve hot with the guacamole dip.

FILLED JACKET POTATOES

Cook these potatoes conventionally, then wrap them in foil and keep them warm at the edge of a barbecue, if wished, ready to fill with a choice of three inspired mixtures.

EACH DRESSING SERVES 4

INGREDIENTS:
4 large or 8 medium baking potatoes
paprika or chilli powder, or chopped
*   fresh herbs, to garnish*

MEXICAN SWEETCORN RELISH:
250 g/8 oz can sweetcorn, drained
½ red (bell) pepper, cored, deseeded and
*   chopped finely*
5 cm/2 inch piece cucumber,
*   chopped finely*
½ tsp chilli powder
salt and pepper

BLUE CHEESE FILLING:
125 g/4 oz/½ cup full-fat soft cheese
125 g/4 oz/½ cup natural
*   fromage frais*
125 g/4 oz Danish blue cheese,
*   cut into cubes*
1 celery stick, chopped finely
2 tsp snipped fresh chives
celery salt and pepper

MUSHROOMS IN SPICY
TOMATO SAUCE:
30 g/1 oz/2 tbsp butter or margarine
250 g/8 oz button mushrooms
150 g/5 oz/⅔ cup natural yogurt
1 tbsp tomato purée (paste)
2 tsp mild curry powder
salt and pepper

1 Scrub the potatoes and prick them with a fork. Bake in a preheated oven at 200°C/400°F/Gas Mark 6 for about 1 hour, until just tender.

2 To make the Mexican Sweetcorn Relish, put half the sweetcorn into a bowl. Put the remainder into a blender or food processor for 10–15 seconds or chop and mash roughly by hand. Add the puréed sweetcorn to the sweetcorn kernels with the (bell) pepper, cucumber and chilli powder. Season to taste. Cover and chill until required.

3 To make the Blue Cheese Filling, mix the soft cheese and fromage frais together until smooth in a large mixing bowl. Add the blue cheese, celery and chives. Season with pepper and celery salt. Cover and chill until required.

4 To make the Mushrooms in Spicy Tomato Sauce, melt the butter in a small frying pan (skillet). Add the mushrooms and cook gently for 3–4 minutes. Remove from the heat and stir in the yogurt, tomato purée (paste) and curry powder. Season to taste.

5 Wrap the cooked potatoes in foil and keep warm at the edge of the barbecue. Serve the fillings sprinkled with paprika, chilli powder or herbs.

JACKET POTATOES WITH BEANS

Baked jacket potatoes, topped with a tasty mixture of beans in a spicy sauce, provide a deliciously filling, high-fibre dish.

SERVES 6

INGREDIENTS:
6 large baking potatoes
4 tbsp vegetable oil or ghee
1 large onion, chopped
2 garlic cloves, crushed
1 tsp ground turmeric
1 tbsp cumin seeds
2 tbsp mild or medium curry paste
350 g/12 oz cherry tomatoes
425 g/14 oz can black-eye beans,
   drained and rinsed
425 g/14 oz can red kidney beans
   (peas), drained and rinsed
1 tbsp lemon juice
2 tbsp tomato purée (paste)
150 ml/¼ pint/⅔ cup water
2 tbsp chopped fresh mint or coriander
   (cilantro)
salt and pepper
sprigs of fresh mint or coriander
   (cilantro), to garnish
natural yogurt, to serve

1 ▼ Wash and scrub the potatoes and prick each one several times with a fork. Place in a preheated oven at 200°C/400°F/Gas Mark 6 for 1–1¼ hours, or until the potatoes feel soft when gently squeezed.

2 ▼ About 20 minutes before the end of cooking time, prepare the topping. Heat the ghee or oil in a saucepan, add the onion and cook gently for 5 minutes, stirring frequently. Add the garlic, turmeric, cumin seeds and curry paste and cook gently for 1 minute.

3 Stir in the tomatoes, black-eye beans (peas) and red kidney beans, lemon juice, tomato purée (paste), water and

chopped mint or coriander (cilantro). Season with salt and pepper, then cover and cook gently for 10 minutes, stirring frequently.

4 ▼ When the potatoes are cooked, cut them in half and mash the flesh lightly with a fork. Spoon the prepared bean mixture on top, garnish with mint or coriander (cilantro) sprigs and serve with the natural yogurt.

SPICY FISH & POTATO CAKES

You need nice, floury-textured old (main crop) potatoes for making these tasty fish cakes. Any white fish of your choice may be used.

SERVES 4

INGREDIENTS:
500 g/1 lb potatoes, peeled and cut into even-sized pieces
500g/1 lb white fish fillets, such as cod or haddock, skinned and boned
6 spring onions (scallions), sliced
1 fresh green chilli, deseeded
2 garlic cloves, peeled
1 tsp salt
1 tbsp medium or hot curry paste
2 eggs, beaten
150 g/5 oz/2½ cups fresh white breadcrumbs
vegetable oil, for shallow frying
mango chutney, to serve

TO GARNISH:
lime wedges
sprigs of fresh coriander (cilantro)

1 ▼ Cook the potatoes in a saucepan of boiling salted water until tender. Drain well, return the potatoes to the saucepan and place over a moderate heat for a few moments to dry the potatoes off.

2 Allow the potatoes to cool slightly, then place in a food processor with the fish, onions, chilli, garlic, salt and curry paste. Process until the ingredients are very finely chopped and blended.

3 ▼ Turn the potato mixture into a bowl and mix in 2 tablespoons of beaten egg and 60 g/2 oz/1 cup of breadcrumbs. Place the remaining beaten egg and breadcrumbs in separate dishes.

4 Divide the fish mixture into 8 and, using a spoon to help you (the mixture is quite soft), dip first in the beaten egg and then coat in the breadcrumbs, and carefully shape the mixture into ovals.

5 ▼ Heat enough vegetable oil in a large frying pan for shallow frying and fry the fish cakes over a moderate heat for 3–4 minutes, turning frequently, until golden brown and cooked through.

6 Drain on absorbent paper towels and garnish with lime wedges and coriander (cilantro) sprigs. Serve the cakes immediately with the mango chutney.

FRITTERS WITH TOMATO RELISH

These are incredibly simple to make and sure to be popular when served as a tempting snack.

MAKES 8

INGREDIENTS:
60 g/2 oz/⅓ cup plain wholemeal (whole wheat) flour
¼ tsp ground coriander
¼ tsp cumin seeds
¼ tsp chilli powder
¼ tsp ground turmeric
¼ tsp salt
1 egg
3 tbsp milk
350 g/12 oz potatoes, peeled
1–2 garlic cloves, crushed
4 spring onions (scallions), trimmed and chopped
60 g/2 oz canned sweetcorn
vegetable oil, for shallow frying

TOMATO RELISH:
1 onion, peeled
250 g/8 oz tomatoes
2 tbsp chopped fresh coriander (cilantro)
2 tbsp chopped fresh mint
2 tbsp lemon juice
¼ tsp roasted cumin seeds
¼ tsp salt
few pinches of chilli powder, to taste

1 ▼ First make the relish. Cut the onion and tomatoes into small dice and place in a bowl with the remaining ingredients. Mix together well and leave for at least 15 minutes before serving to allow the flavours to blend.

2 ▲ Place the flour in a bowl, stir in the coriander, cumin, chilli powder, turmeric and salt and make a well in the centre. Add the egg and milk and mix to form a fairly thick batter.

3 Coarsely grate the potatoes, place in a sieve and rinse well under cold running water. Drain and squeeze dry, then stir into the batter with the garlic, spring onions (scallions) and sweetcorn.

4 ▲ Heat about 5 mm/¼ inch oil in a large frying pan (skillet) and add a few tablespoonfuls of the mixture at a time, flattening each one to form a thin cake. Fry gently for 2–3 minutes or until golden brown and cooked through, turning frequently.

5 Drain on paper towels and keep hot while frying the remaining mixture in the same way. Serve hot with the tomato relish.

SWEETCORN FRITTERS

An ideal supper dish for two, or for one if you halve the quantities. You can use the remaining sweetcorn in another recipe.

SERVES 2

INGREDIENTS:
2 tbsp oil
1 small onion, sliced thinly
1 garlic clove, crushed
350 g/12 oz potatoes
200 g/7 oz can sweetcorn, drained
¼ tsp dried oregano
1 egg, beaten
60 g/2 oz/½ cup Edam or Gouda
  cheese, grated
salt and pepper
2–4 eggs
2–4 tomatoes, sliced
sprigs of fresh parsley, to garnish

1 Heat 1 tablespoon of the oil in a non-stick frying pan (skillet). Add the onion and garlic, and fry very gently until soft, but only lightly coloured, stirring frequently. Remove from the heat.

2 ▲ Grate the potatoes coarsely into a bowl and mix in the sweetcorn, oregano, beaten egg and seasoning. Add the fried onion.

3 ▼ Heat the remaining oil in the frying pan (skillet). Divide the potato mixture in half and add to the pan to make 2 oval-shaped cakes, levelling and shaping the cakes with a palette knife (spatula).

4 Cook gently for about 10 minutes until browned underneath and almost cooked through, keeping in shape with the palette knife (spatula) and loosening so they don't stick.

5 ▼ Sprinkle each fritter with the grated cheese and place under a preheated moderately hot grill (broiler) until golden brown.

6 Meanwhile, poach either 1 or 2 eggs for each person until just cooked. Transfer the fritters to warmed plates and top each fritter with the eggs and sliced tomatoes. Garnish with the fresh parsley and serve at once while still hot.

GOLDEN CHEESE & LEEK POTATO CAKES

Make these tasty potato cakes for a quick and simple supper dish. Serve them with scrambled eggs if you are very hungry.

SERVES 4

INGREDIENTS:
1 kg/2 lb potatoes
4 tbsp milk
60 g/2 oz/¼ cup butter or margarine
2 leeks, chopped finely
1 onion, chopped finely
175 g/6 oz/1½ cups grated Caerphilly or Cheddar cheese
1 tbsp chopped fresh parsley or chives
1 egg, beaten
2 tbsp water
90 g/3 oz/1½ cups fresh white or brown breadcrumbs
vegetable oil, for shallow frying
salt and pepper
sprigs of flat-leaf parsley, to garnish
mixed salad, to serve

1 ▼ Cook the potatoes in lightly salted boiling water until tender. Drain and mash them with the milk and the butter or margarine.

2 Cook the leeks and onion in a small amount of salted boiling water for about 10 minutes until tender. Drain.

3 ▼ In a large mixing bowl, combine the leeks and onion with the mashed potato, cheese and parsley or chives. Season to taste.

4 Beat together the egg and water in a shallow bowl. Sprinkle the breadcrumbs into a separate shallow bowl. Shape the potato mixture into 12 even-sized cakes, brushing each with the egg mixture, then coating with the breadcrumbs.

5 ▲ Heat the oil in a large frying pan (skillet) and fry the potato cakes gently for about 2–3 minutes on each side until lightly golden. Garnish with parsley and serve with a salad.

ROSTI POTATO CAKE WITH COURGETTES (ZUCCHINI) & CARROTS

A mixture of coarsely grated potatoes, courgettes (zucchini) and carrots with fried sliced onions is cooked into a cake in a large frying pan (skillet) and topped with cheese, then finished off under the grill (broiler). Serve warm or cold, cut into wedges.

SERVES 6

INGREDIENTS:
2 tbsp vegetable oil
1 large onion, sliced thinly
1 garlic clove, crushed (optional)
1 kg/2 lb potatoes
175 g/6 oz courgettes (zucchini), trimmed
125 g/4 oz carrots
¼ tsp ground coriander
60 g/2 oz/½ cup mature (sharp) Gouda or Cheddar cheese, grated (optional)
salt and pepper

1 Heat 1 tablespoon of the oil in a large frying pan (skillet), add the onion and garlic, if using, and fry gently for about 5 minutes, until soft but only barely coloured.

2 ▼ Grate the potatoes coarsely into a bowl. Grate the courgettes (zucchini) and carrots, and mix into the potatoes with the coriander and seasoning until evenly mixed, then add the fried onions.

3 ▼ Heat the remaining oil in the frying pan (skillet), add the potato mixture and cook gently, stirring occasionally, for about 5 minutes. Flatten down into a cake and cook gently for 6–8 minutes, until browned underneath and almost cooked through.

4 ▼ Sprinkle the top of the potato cake with the grated cheese, if using, and place under a preheated moderate grill (broiler) for about 5 minutes, or until lightly browned and cooked through.

5 Loosen the potato cake with a large palette knife (spatula) and slip it carefully on to a plate. Leave until cold, then cover with clingfilm (plastic wrap) or foil and chill until required. Serve cut into wedges.

FISH CAKES WITH SPICY SAUCE

A smoky flavour gives these fish cakes a special tang, making them very popular with children and adults alike. The spicy sauce is a good way to liven up bottled ketchup.

SERVES 4

INGREDIENTS:
1 kg/2 lb potatoes, cut into chunks
350–500 g/¾–1 lb smoked haddock or cod fillet, skinned
1 bay leaf
2 hard-boiled (hard-cooked) eggs, chopped finely
2–3 tbsp chopped fresh parsley
1 tbsp chopped fresh tarragon, or 1 tsp dried tarragon
2–3 spring onions (scallions), chopped (optional)
30 g/1 oz/2 tbsp butter or margarine
1 egg, beaten
dried white or golden breadcrumbs
salt and pepper
vegetable oil, for brushing or frying

SPICY SAUCE:
150 ml/¼ pint/⅔ cup dry white wine
150 ml/¼ pint/⅔ cup tomato ketchup
1–2 garlic cloves, crushed
good dash of Worcestershire sauce

TO GARNISH:
sprigs of fresh parsley
lemon slices

1 Cook the potatoes in boiling salted water until tender.

2 Meanwhile, put the fish and bay leaf in a saucepan and barely cover with water. Bring to the boil, cover and simmer for 15 minutes until tender.

3 ▼ Drain the fish, remove the skin and any bones and flake. Put in a bowl with the eggs, herbs, spring onions (scallions), if using, and seasoning and mix well.

4 ▼ Drain the potatoes and mash with the butter and seasoning. Add to the fish and mix thoroughly.

5 ▲ Divide the mixture into 8 and shape into cakes. Brush with beaten egg then coat in breadcrumbs. Put on a greased baking sheet, brush with oil and cook in a preheated oven at 200°C/400°F/Gas Mark 6 for about 30 minutes until golden. Alternatively, fry for about 5 minutes on each side.

6 To make the spicy sauce, put all the ingredients in a saucepan, bring to the boil and simmer, uncovered, for about 15 minutes until thickened and smooth. Adjust the seasoning. Garnish the fish cakes with parsley and lemon and serve with the sauce.

FLAMENCO EGGS

This Spanish-style egg recipe is full of lively colours and flavours.

SERVES 4

INGREDIENTS:
6 tbsp olive oil
2 thick slices white bread, cut into cubes
500 g/1 lb potatoes, cut into small cubes
1 onion, chopped
60 g/2 oz green beans, cut into ½ cm/ 1 inch lengths
2 small courgettes (zucchini), halved and sliced
1 red (bell) pepper, cored, deseeded and chopped
4 tomatoes, deseeded and sliced
2 chorizo sausages, sliced
chilli powder, to taste
4 eggs
salt
chopped fresh parsley, to garnish

1 ▼ Heat the oil in a large frying pan (skillet) and add the cubes of bread. Fry until golden brown, then remove with a perforated spoon and drain on paper towels. Set aside.

2 Add the potatoes to the frying pan (skillet) and cook over a low heat, turning often, for about 15 minutes until just tender.

3 ▼ Add the onion to the frying pan (skillet) and cook for 3 minutes, then add the green beans, courgettes (zucchini), (bell) pepper and tomatoes. Cook gently for 3–4 minutes, stirring often. Stir in the chorizo sausage. Season with salt and a little chilli powder.

4 ▼ Grease 4 individual ovenproof dishes or 1 large ovenproof dish with olive oil. Transfer the vegetable mixture to the dishes and make a hollow in the mixture. Carefully crack 1 egg into each hollow. Bake in a preheated oven at 190°C/375°F/ Gas Mark 5 for 10 minutes.

5 Sprinkle the cubes of fried bread over the surface and bake for a further 2 minutes. Serve immediately, garnished with chopped fresh parsley.

SPANISH OMELETTE

Use any leftover cooked pasta you may have, such as penne, short-cut macaroni or shells, to make this fluffy omelette an instant success.

SERVES 2

INGREDIENTS
4 tbsp olive oil
1 small Spanish onion, chopped
1 fennel bulb, thinly sliced
125 g/4 oz raw potato, diced and dried
1 garlic clove, chopped
4 eggs
1 tbsp chopped fresh parsley
pinch of chilli powder
90 g/3 oz short pasta, cooked weight
1 tbsp stuffed green olives, halved, plus extra to garnish
salt and pepper
sprigs of fresh marjoram, to garnish
tomato salad, to serve

1 Heat 2 tablespoons of the oil in a heavy frying pan (skillet) over a low heat and fry the onion, fennel and potato for 8–10 minutes, stirring occasionally, until the potato is just tender. Stir in the garlic and cook for 1 minute. Remove from the heat, lift out the vegetables with a perforated spoon and set aside. Rinse and dry the pan.

2 Break the eggs into a bowl and beat them until they are frothy. Stir in the parsley and season with salt, pepper and chilli powder.

3 ▼ Heat 1 tablespoon of the remaining oil in a pan over a medium

heat. Pour in half the beaten eggs, then add the cooked vegetables, the pasta and the green olives. Pour on the remaining egg and cook until the sides begin to set.

4 ▲ Lift up the edges with a spatula to allow the uncooked egg to spread underneath. Continue cooking the omelette, shaking the pan occasionally, until the underside is golden brown.

5 ▼ Slide the omelette out on to a large, flat plate and wipe the pan clean with paper towels. Heat the remaining oil in the pan and invert the omelette. Cook on the other side until brown.

6 Slide the omelette on to a warmed serving dish. Garnish with a few olives and the marjoram sprigs, and serve hot, cut into wedges and accompanied by a tomato salad.

PICNIC OMELETTE SQUARES

An oven-baked omelette with diced potatoes, onions, peas, tomatoes, herbs and cheese is cut into small bite-sized squares that are perfect for picnics.

MAKES ABOUT 36 SQUARES

INGREDIENTS:
2 tbsp olive oil
1 onion, thinly sliced
1 garlic clove, crushed
1 courgette (zucchini), trimmed and grated coarsely
1 red, green or orange (bell) pepper, halved, cored and deseeded
175 g/6 oz/1 cup cooked potato, diced
90 g/3 oz/⅔ cup cooked peas
2 tomatoes, skinned, deseeded and cut into strips
2 tsp chopped fresh mixed herbs, or 1 tsp dried mixed herbs
6 eggs
45–60 g/1½–2 oz/⅓–½ cup Gruyère or fresh Parmesan cheese, grated
salt and pepper

1 Heat the oil in a large frying pan (skillet) and fry the onion and garlic very gently for about 5 minutes, until soft but not coloured. Add the courgette (zucchini) and fry for a further 1–2 minutes. Turn into a bowl.

2 Place the (bell) pepper on a grill (broiler) rack skin-side upwards and cook under a preheated moderate grill (broiler) until the skin is well charred. Leave to cool slightly, then peel off the blackened skin and slice or chop the (bell) pepper flesh. Add the (bell) pepper to the onion mixture, together with the potato, peas, tomatoes and herbs.

3 ▲ Beat the eggs together with 1–2 tablespoons water and seasoning, then add to the vegetables and mix.

4 ▼ Line a shallow 20–23 cm/8–9 inch square cake tin (pan) with non-stick

baking parchment. Do not cut into the corners, just fold the parchment. Pour in the egg mixture, making sure the vegetables are fairly evenly distributed.

5 Cook in a preheated oven at 180°C/350°F/Gas Mark 4 for about 15 minutes or until almost set.

6 ▲ Sprinkle with the cheese and either return to the oven for 5–10 minutes or place under a preheated moderate grill (broiler) until evenly browned. Leave to cool. Remove from the tin (pan), cut into 2.5–4 cm/ 1–1½ inch squares and serve immediately or pack for a picnic.

CORNISH PASTIES

Cornish pasties were originally made for miners' lunches, which makes them ideal for picnics and packed lunches. For a variation on this recipe, add 1 small chopped carrot to the meat mixture; lamb can also be substituted for the beef in the recipe.

SERVES 4

INGREDIENTS:
350 g/12 oz lean braising steak
125 g/4 oz raw potato, peeled
1 onion
salt and pepper
milk, for brushing

PASTRY:
350 g/12oz/3 cups plain (all-purpose)
  flour
½ tsp salt
175 g/6 oz/¾ cup margarine, cut into
  small pieces
chilled water, to mix

1 ▼ First make the pastry. Sift the flour and salt into a large bowl. Add the margarine and rub in (cut in) until the mixture resembles fine breadcrumbs. Add sufficient cold water to make a soft, but not sticky, dough. Knead lightly for a few moments, then wrap in clingfilm (plastic wrap) and chill for 10–15 minutes.

2 ▼ Divide the dough into 4 pieces. Roll out each piece on a lightly floured work surface (counter) to a diameter of about 20 cm/8 inches.

3 Cut the steak into small pieces, dice the potato and chop the onion. Mix together in a bowl and season well with salt and pepper.

4 ▲ Divide the meat mixture equally between the rounds. Dampen the edges with a little water and draw the edges together to form a seam across the top. Crimp the short ends.

5 Place the pasties on a baking sheet and brush with a little milk. Bake in a preheated oven at 220°C/425°F/ Gas Mark 7 for 15 minutes, then reduce to 160°C/ 325°F/Gas Mark 3, cover with foil to prevent them from becoming too brown, and bake for a further hour. Serve warm or cold.

ALMOND POTATO BITES

In this recipe creamy mashed potatoes are coated in crunchy almonds, then fried until golden brown. Serve the potato bites as a party dish, or as a side dish with a special meal.

SERVES 4

INGREDIENTS:
*1 kg/2 lb old (main crop) potatoes,
    peeled and quartered
60 g/2 oz/¼ cup butter
2 tbsp milk
1 egg, beaten
salt and pepper
vegetable oil, for frying*

TO COAT:
*60 g/2 oz/½ cup plain (all-purpose)
    flour
salt and pepper
1 egg
2 tbsp cold water
90 g/3 oz/⅔ cup blanched almonds,
    finely chopped*

1 Cook the potatoes in plenty of lightly salted boiling water for 15–20 minutes until tender. Drain well and mash until no large lumps remain.

2 ▼ Add the butter and milk to the potatoes, beating well with a wooden spoon or hand-held electric beater. Mix in the beaten egg and season with salt and pepper.

3 Shape the potato mixture into 20 equally sized small balls or cakes.

4 ▼ Season the flour with salt and pepper and sprinkle on a flat plate. In a shallow bowl, beat the egg with the cold water. Put the almonds into a separate shallow bowl. Dip the potato balls into the flour, then into the egg and finally into the almonds to coat evenly.

5 ▲ Pour the vegetable oil into a deep frying pan (skillet) or wok to a depth of 1 cm/½ inch and heat until a cube of bread browns in 30 seconds. Fry the potato balls in batches for 2–3 minutes, turning often, until golden brown. Lift out with a slotted spoon, drain on paper towels and serve while hot.

ROOT VEGETABLE CRISPS WITH CREAMY GARLIC DIP

These crispy root vegetables taste superb and make an excellent nibble to serve with drinks.

SERVES 4

INGREDIENTS:
1 large potato, scrubbed
2 large parsnips, scrubbed
175 g/6 oz sweet potato, scrubbed
175 g/6 oz celeriac (celery root), scrubbed
175 g/6 oz raw beetroot, scrubbed
vegetable oil, for deep frying
salt and pepper

GARLIC DIP:
2 garlic cloves
3–4 spring onions (scallions), trimmed
few sprigs of mixed fresh herbs, such as parsley, chives, dill, marjoram or thyme
300 ml/½ pint/1¼ cups soured cream
salt and pepper

1 ▼ Cut all the vegetables into very thin slices, without peeling them. If preferred, this can be done using a food processor or mandoline. Keep the different vegetables in separate batches.

2 Pour the vegetable oil into a deep-fat fryer or wok to a depth of 7–10 cm/3–4 inches. Heat to 180–190°C/350–375°F, or until a cube of bread browns in 30 seconds. Fry the vegetables in batches for several minutes until crisp and browned, cooking the beetroot last of all to prevent the oil from discolouring. Lift the cooked crisps from the oil with a perforated spoon and drain on paper towels. Leave to cool.

3 ▼ Make the dip. Peel and crush the garlic cloves. Finely chop the spring onions (scallions) and herbs.

4 ▲ Put the soured cream in a small mixing bowl and add the garlic, spring onion (scallion) and herbs. Season well with salt and pepper. Transfer to a serving bowl, cover and chill until ready to serve.

5 Sprinkle the vegetable crisps with salt and pepper and serve with the creamy garlic dip.

SIDE DISHES

Although potatoes are one of the most popular side dishes, there are many more imaginative ways of serving them than most people realize. Potatoes can be cooked and served in many different ways, such as mashing, roasting, stir-frying, pan-frying, deep-frying, baking and boiling. Some exotic or ethnic-style potato dishes combine well with simply cooked main courses, like grilled (broiled) fish or chicken, and they can add extra interest to a meal. In this chapter, you will find recipes for all kinds of side dishes, from mash, French fries and new potato or baked potato recipes to Indian-style side dishes such as Aloo Chat and Bombay Potatoes, along with the classic French recipe Potatoes Lyonnaise. There are great ideas for adding excitement to old favourites, such as Leek, Mustard & Crispy Bacon Mash or Lemony New Potatoes. There are also recipes for sweet potatoes, such as Sautéed Sweet Potatoes with Rosemary. Be creative when serving different dishes together, and don't be afraid to combine some of the more exotic recipes with dishes from other culinary traditions.

SPICY INDIAN-STYLE POTATOES

Potatoes cooked this way are so delicious, yet quick and simple to prepare. Cut the potatoes into similar-sized pieces to make sure they cook evenly.

SERVES 4

INGREDIENTS:
750 g/1½ lb potatoes
salt
60 g/2 oz/¼ cup ghee or clarified butter
2 tbsp vegetable oil
1 tsp ground turmeric
1 large onion, peeled, quartered and sliced
2–3 garlic cloves, crushed
5 cm/2 inch piece ginger root, peeled and chopped
1½ tsp cumin seeds
¼–½ tsp chilli powder
2 tsp lemon juice
1 tbsp shredded fresh mint leaves
sprigs of fresh mint, to garnish

1 ▼ Peel the potatoes and cut into 2–2.5 cm/¾–1 inch cubes and cook in a pan of boiling, salted water for 6–8 minutes or until knife-tip tender (do not overcook). Drain well, return to the pan and shake dry over a moderate heat for a few moments.

2 ▲ Heat the ghee or butter and oil in a large frying pan (skillet) over a medium heat. Stir in the turmeric, then add the sliced onion and the cooked potatoes and fry for 4–5 minutes or until the mixture is beginning to brown, stirring and turning the vegetables frequently.

3 ▼ Stir in the garlic, ginger, cumin seeds, chilli powder and salt to taste. Fry over gentle heat for 1 minute, stirring all the time.

4 Transfer the potatoes to a warm serving dish. Add the lemon juice to the juices in the pan and spoon the mixture over the potatoes. Sprinkle with the shredded mint leaves, garnish with sprigs of mint and serve hot.

MIXED VEGETABLE BHAJI

*In this delicious dish, the vegetables
are first parboiled and then lightly
braised with onions, tomatoes and
spices.*

SERVES 4–6

INGREDIENTS:

1 small cauliflower
125 g/4 oz French (green) beans
2 potatoes
4 tbsp ghee or vegetable oil
1 onion, chopped
2 garlic cloves, crushed
*5 cm/2 inch piece ginger root, peeled
    and cut into fine slivers*
1 tsp cumin seeds
2 tbsp medium curry paste
425 g/14 oz can chopped tomatoes
150 ml/¼ pint/⅔ cup water
4 tbsp strained thick yogurt
*chopped fresh coriander (cilantro),
    to garnish*

1 ▼ Break the cauliflower into neat
florets. Top, tail and halve the beans.
Peel and quarter the potatoes
lengthways, then cut each quarter into
3 pieces. Cook all the prepared
vegetables in a saucepan of boiling,
salted water for 8 minutes. Drain well,
return to the pan and shake dry over a
low heat for a few moments.

2 ▼ Heat the ghee or oil in a large
frying pan (skillet), add the onion,
garlic, ginger and cumin seeds and
stir-fry gently for 3 minutes. Stir in the
curry paste, tomatoes and water and
bring to the boil. Reduce the heat
and simmer the spicy mixture for
2 minutes.

3 ▼ Stir in the parboiled vegetables
and mix lightly. Cover and cook
gently for 5–8 minutes until just
tender and cooked through. Whisk the
yogurt to soften and drizzle the
vegetable mixture with the yogurt.
Sprinkle with the chopped coriander
(cilantro). Serve hot.

FRIED SPICED POTATOES

These spicy potatoes make a super accompaniment to almost any main course dish, though they are rather high in calories!

SERVES 4–6

INGREDIENTS:
2 onions, peeled and quartered
5 cm/2 inch piece ginger root, peeled
  and finely chopped
2 garlic cloves, peeled
2–3 tbsp mild or medium curry paste
4 tbsp water
750 g/1½ lb new potatoes
vegetable oil, for deep frying
3 tbsp vegetable ghee or oil
150 ml/¼ pint/⅔ cup strained thick
  natural yogurt
150 ml/¼ pint/⅔ cup double (heavy)
  cream
3 tbsp chopped fresh mint
salt and pepper
¼ bunch spring onions (scallions),
  trimmed and chopped, to garnish

1 ▼ Place the onions, ginger, garlic, curry paste and water in a blender or food processor and process until smooth, scraping down the sides of the machine, and blending again, if necessary.

2 Cut the potatoes into quarters – the pieces need to be about 2.5 cm/ 1 inch in size – and pat dry with paper towels. Heat the oil in a deep-fat fryer to 180°C/350°F/Gas Mark 4, or until a cube of bread browns in 30 seconds. Fry the potatoes, in batches, for about 5 minutes or until golden brown, turning frequently. Remove and drain on paper towels.

3 ▼ Heat the ghee or oil in a large frying pan (skillet), add the curry and onion mixture and fry gently for 2 minutes, stirring all the time. Add the yogurt, cream and 2 tablespoons of the fresh mint. Mix well.

4 ▼ Add the fried potatoes and stir until coated in the sauce. Cook for a further 5–7 minutes, or until heated through and sauce has thickened, stirring frequently.

5 Season with salt and pepper to taste and sprinkle with the remaining mint and sliced spring onions (scallions). Serve immediately.

CURRIED ROAST POTATOES

This is the kind of Indian-inspired dish that would fit easily into any Western menu. Delicious on a buffet, or a surprise accompaniment to a traditional roast dinner, it would also be good served with a curry in place of the more traditional rice.

SERVES 4

INGREDIENTS:
2 tsp cumin seeds
2 tsp coriander seeds
90 g/3 oz/⅓ cup salted butter
1 tsp ground turmeric
1 tsp black mustard seeds
2 garlic cloves, crushed
2 dried red chillies
750 g/1½ lb baby new potatoes

1 ▼ Grind the cumin and coriander seeds together in a pestle and mortar or spice grinder. Grinding them fresh like this captures all of the flavour before it has a chance to dry out.

2 Melt the butter gently in a roasting tin (pan) and add the turmeric, mustard seeds, garlic and chillies and the ground cumin and coriander seeds. Stir well to combine evenly. Place in a preheated oven at 200°C/400°F/Gas Mark 6 for 5 minutes.

3 ▼ Remove the tin (pan) from the oven – the spices should be very fragrant at this stage – and add the potatoes. Stir well so that the butter and spice mix coats the potatoes completely.

4 ▲ Put back in the preheated oven and bake for 20–25 minutes, stirring occasionally. Test the potatoes with a skewer – if they drop off the end of the skewer when lifted, they are done. Serve immediately.

ALOO CHAT

Aloo Chat (chat means salad) is one of a variety of Indian foods served at any time of the day. Indians are expert at combining flavours and textures in subtle mixes designed to satisfy and stimulate the appetite. This makes an exciting side dish that can be served with all manner of dishes, not just Indian food.

SERVES 4

INGREDIENTS:

125 g/4 oz/generous ¾ cup chick-peas (garbanzo beans), soaked overnight in cold water and drained
1 dried red chilli
500 g/1 lb waxy potatoes, such as red-skinned or Cyprus potatoes, boiled in their skins and peeled
1 tsp cumin seeds
1 tsp black peppercorns
2 tsp salt
¼ tsp dried mint
¼ tsp chilli powder
¼ tsp ground ginger
2 tsp mango powder
120 ml/4 fl oz/½ cup natural yogurt
vegetable oil, for deep frying
4 poppadoms

1 ▼ Boil the chick-peas (garbanzo beans) with the chilli in plenty of water for about 1 hour until tender. Drain well.

2 ▲ Cut the potatoes into 2.5 cm/ 1 inch dice and mix into the chick-peas (garbanzo beans) while they are still warm. Set aside.

3 Grind together the cumin, peppercorns and salt in a spice grinder or pestle and mortar. Stir in the dried mint, chilli powder, ginger and mango powder.

4 ▼ Put a small dry saucepan or frying pan (skillet) over a low heat and add the spice mix. Stir until fragrant and immediately remove from the heat.

5 Stir half of the spice mix into the chick-peas (garbanzo beans) and potatoes, and stir the yogurt into the other half.

6 Cook the poppadoms according to the packet instructions. Drain on plenty of paper towels. Break into bite-sized pieces and stir into the potatoes and chick-peas (garbanzo beans). Spoon over the spiced yogurt and serve immediately.

BOMBAY POTATOES

Although virtually unknown in India, this dish is a very popular item on Indian restaurant menus in other parts of the world. It works best when served with rice as a vegetable dish, rather than instead of rice. The success of the recipe rests on using waxy potatoes, such as red-skinned or Cyprus potatoes, because they do not break up readily. Panch poran spice mix, which includes cumin, fennel, nigella and fenugreek, can be bought from Asian or Indian food shops.

SERVES 4

INGREDIENTS:
1 kg/2 lb waxy potatoes, peeled
2 tbsp ghee
1 tsp panch poran spice mix
3 tsp ground turmeric
2 tbsp tomato purée (paste)
300 ml/½ pint/1¼ cups natural yogurt
salt
chopped fresh coriander (cilantro),
  to garnish

1 Put the whole potatoes into a large saucepan of salted cold water, bring to the boil, then simmer until the potatoes are just cooked but not tender; the time depends on the size of the potato, but an average-sized one should take about 15 minutes.

2 ▲ Put the ghee into a saucepan over a medium heat, and add the panch poran, turmeric, tomato purée (paste), yogurt and salt. Bring to the boil, and simmer, uncovered, for 5 minutes.

3 ▲ Drain the potatoes and cut each into 4 pieces.

4 ▼ Add the potatoes to the pan and cook with a lid on. Transfer to an ovenproof casserole, cover and cook in a preheated oven at 180°C/350°F/ Gas Mark 4 for about 40 minutes, until the potatoes are tender and the sauce has thickened a little.

5 Sprinkle with fresh chopped coriander (cilantro) and serve.

MUSTARD & ONION POTATOES

Mustard seeds give the potatoes a nutty taste. This dish can be served with any type of main course, and is especially good served with curries or with barbecued kebabs in the summer.

SERVES 4

INGREDIENTS:
350 g/12 oz small new potatoes
3 tbsp oil
2 tbsp brown mustard seeds
1 tsp cumin seeds
1 tsp crushed dried red chillies
250 g/8 oz baby onions
1 garlic clove, chopped
1 cm/⅟₄ inch piece ginger root
⅟₄ tsp garam masala

1 ▲ Boil the potatoes in salted water for 10–15 minutes until just tender. Drain the potatoes, cut in half if they are large, and set aside.

2 ▼ Heat the oil in a Balti pan or wok, add the mustard seeds, cumin and chillies and fry until the seeds start to pop.

3 ▼ Add the onions to the pan and stir-fry until golden brown. Add the garlic and ginger and stir-fry for 1 minute longer.

4 ▼ Stir in the potatoes and garam masala and stir-fry for 4–5 minutes until the potatoes are golden brown. Serve hot.

POTATOES LYONNAISE

In this classic French recipe, sliced potatoes are cooked with onions to make a delicious accompaniment to a main meal. If you find that the potatoes blacken slightly as they boil, add a teaspoonful of lemon juice to the cooking water.

SERVES 4

INGREDIENTS
1.25 kg/2½ lb old (main crop) potatoes, peeled
4 tbsp olive oil
30 g/1 oz/2 tbsp butter
2 onions, sliced
2–3 garlic cloves, crushed (optional)
salt and pepper
chopped fresh parsley, to garnish

1 Slice the potatoes into 5 mm/¼ inch slices. Put in a large saucepan of lightly salted water and bring to the boil. Cover and simmer gently for 10–12 minutes until just tender. Avoid boiling too rapidly or the potatoes will break up and lose their shape. When cooked, drain well.

2 ▲ While the potatoes are cooking, heat the oil and butter in a very large frying pan (skillet) and gently fry the onions and the garlic, if using, until the onions are softened.

3 ▼ Add the cooked potatoes to the frying pan (skillet) and cook with the onions, stirring occasionally, for 5–8 minutes until the potatoes are well-browned.

4 ▲ Season well. Sprinkle over the chopped parsley to serve. If wished, transfer the potatoes and onions to a large ovenproof dish and keep warm in a low oven until ready to serve.

LEMONY NEW POTATOES & HERBY NEW POTATOES

Choose from these two divine recipes for new potatoes. To check that new potatoes are fresh, rub the skin; the skin will come off easily if fresh.

SERVES 4

LEMONY NEW POTATO INGREDIENTS:

1 kg/2 lb new potatoes
45 g/1½ oz/3 tbsp butter
1 tbsp finely grated lemon rind
2 tbsp lemon juice
1 tbsp chopped fresh dill or chives
salt and pepper
extra chopped fresh dill or chives,
  to garnish

1 ▼ Either scrub the potatoes well or remove skins by scraping off with a sharp knife. Cook the potatoes in plenty of lightly salted boiling water for about 15 minutes until just tender.

2 ▼ While the potatoes are cooking, melt the butter over a low heat. Add the lemon rind, juice and herbs. Season with salt and pepper.

3 Drain the cooked potatoes and transfer to a serving bowl. Pour over the lemony butter mixture and stir gently to mix. Garnish with extra herbs and serve hot or warm.

HERBY NEW POTATO INGREDIENTS:

1 kg/2 lb new potatoes
3 tbsp light olive oil
1½ tbsp white wine vinegar
pinch of dry mustard
pinch of caster (superfine) sugar
salt and pepper
2 tbsp chopped mixed fresh herbs, such
  as parsley, chives, marjoram, basil
  and rosemary
extra chopped fresh mixed herbs,
  to garnish

1 Prepare and cook the potatoes as described in step 1 above.

2 While the potatoes are cooking, whisk the oil, vinegar, mustard, caster (superfine) sugar and seasoning together in a small bowl. Add the chopped herbs and mix well to combine.

3 ▲ Drain the potatoes and pour over the oil and vinegar mixture, stirring to coat evenly.

4 Transfer to a serving bowl. Garnish with extra fresh herbs and serve the potatoes warm or cold.

GARLIC MASH WITH MELTED CHEESE & LEEK, MUSTARD & CRISPY BACON MASH

Creamy mashed potato is a favourite with so many meals. Here are two versions to try.

SERVES 4

MELTED CHEESE INGREDIENTS:

1 kg/2 lb old (main crop) potatoes, peeled
salt and pepper
30 g/1 oz/2 tbsp butter
1–2 garlic cloves, crushed
4 tbsp milk
90 g/3 oz mozzarella or Cheddar cheese, grated

1 Cut the potatoes into quarters and cook in lightly salted boiling water for about 20 minutes until tender. Drain well, mash and season.

2 ▲ Melt the butter in a small frying pan (skillet) and gently fry the garlic for about 3 minutes, until softened. Add to the potatoes with the milk and beat well with a wooden spoon, or use a hand-held electric mixer, until smooth and creamy.

3 ▼ Transfer to a greased ovenproof dish. Sprinkle with the cheese and bake in a preheated oven at 180°C/ 350°F/Gas Mark 4 for 15–20 minutes.

LEEK, MUSTARD AND CRISPY BACON INGREDIENTS:

1 kg/2 lb old (main crop) potatoes, peeled
salt and pepper
30 g/1 oz/2 tbsp butter
1 large leek, chopped
2 tsp coarse-grain mustard
4 slices streaky bacon
chopped fresh parsley, to garnish

1 Prepare, boil and mash the potatoes as described for the Garlic Mash with Melted Cheese, seasoning well with salt and pepper.

2 ▲ Melt the butter in a small frying pan (skillet) and gently fry the leek until softened. Add to the mash with the mustard. Transfer to a greased ovenproof dish and bake in a preheated oven at 180°C/ 350°F/ Gas Mark 4 for 15–20 minutes.

3 While cooking, grill (broil) the bacon under a preheated hot grill (broiler) until crisp. Remove, drain on paper towels and snip into bacon bits. Scatter the bacon and parsley over the mash and serve.

FLUFFY BAKED POTATOES

With just a little extra effort baked potatoes can taste magnificent! Chopped red (bell) pepper and drained canned sweetcorn can be used instead of ham for a vegetarian alternative.

SERVES 4

INGREDIENTS:
4 large baking potatoes, scrubbed
30 g/1 oz cooked ham, chopped
125 g/4 oz Cheddar or red Leicester
  cheese, grated
2 tsp coarse-grain mustard
2 eggs, separated
salt and pepper
sprigs of fresh parsley, to garnish

1 Use a fork to prick the potatoes 2 or 3 times to prevent them from bursting. Bake in a preheated oven at 200°C/400°F/Gas Mark 6 for about 1 hour, until tender. Alternatively, cook for 10–12 minutes in a microwave oven on high. Cool the potatoes for a few minutes.

2 ▲ Halve the potatoes and carefully scoop out the flesh into a large bowl, taking care to avoid damaging the skins. Mash the potato flesh by hand with a fork or masher until no large lumps remain.

3 ▼ Mix the ham, cheese, mustard and egg yolks into the mashed potato, stirring well to combine. Season with salt and pepper.

4 ▲ Whisk the egg whites in a bowl until stiff. Using a large metal spoon, gently fold the egg whites into the potato mixture.

5 Spoon the mixture back into the potato skins and place in a shallow greased baking dish. Bake for a further 15–20 minutes until the potatoes are set and golden brown on top. Garnish with the parsley sprigs and serve.

SAUTÉED SWEET POTATOES WITH ROSEMARY

Sweet potatoes are used in this recipe to make a tasty side dish, but you can substitute ordinary potatoes if desired.

SERVES 4

INGREDIENTS:
150 ml/¼ pint/⅔ cup single (light) cream
1 tsp lemon juice
1 tbsp snipped fresh chives
1 kg/2 lb sweet potatoes, scrubbed
1 tsp salt
4 tbsp olive oil
15 g/½ oz/1 tbsp butter
1 tbsp chopped fresh rosemary
¼ tsp allspice
salt and pepper
sprigs of fresh rosemary, to garnish

1 Pour the cream into a small serving bowl. Stir in the lemon juice to combine. Cover and chill for 20–30 minutes to 'sour' the cream. Add the chives and stir to mix. Refrigerate until ready to serve.

2 ▼ Put the sweet potatoes into a large saucepan of cold water. Add the salt and bring to the boil. Cover, reduce the heat and simmer for about 15 minutes until just tender. Drain well, then peel and dice.

3 ▼ Heat the oil and butter in a large frying pan (skillet) and add the diced sweet potatoes. Gently fry the potatoes over a medium heat for about 8 minutes, stirring occasionally, until golden brown.

4 ▲ Add the rosemary to the sweet potatoes. Season the mixture with allspice, salt and pepper. Garnish with sprigs of rosemary and serve while hot, accompanied by the soured cream.

FRENCH FRIES

This recipe makes perfect French fries – light, crisp and golden brown. You may like to use a mandoline or food processor to cut the potatoes into different shapes for added interest. Unpeeled potatoes can also be used; just scrub well before cutting to size.

SERVES 4

INGREDIENTS:
1 kg/2 lb old (main crop) potatoes, peeled
vegetable oil, for frying
salt and pepper

1 Cut the potatoes into 1 cm/½ inch slices, and then into 1 cm/½ inch wide strips. Rinse well in cold water, drain thoroughly and pat dry with paper towels. (If preparing in advance, place the cut potatoes in a large bowl and cover with cold water until ready to cook.)

2 ▲ Add the vegetable oil to a depth of 7–10 cm/3–4 inches in a deep-fat fryer. Heat to a temperature of 180–190°C /350–375°F. To test that the oil is hot enough, add one potato slice; it should rise to the surface, surrounded by bubbles, when the oil is hot enough. Add potatoes to quarter-fill the wire basket. Carefully lower into the oil and cook for about 6 minutes.

3 ▼ Lift the wire basket from the oil and drain for a few seconds. Remove the French fries and drain on paper towels. Repeat the procedure until all the potatoes are cooked.

4 ▲ Just before serving, reheat the oil and deep fry the fries for a further 3–4 minutes until crisp and golden brown. Drain well on paper towels, season with salt and pepper and serve at once.

MAIN MEALS

Potatoes find their way into almost every meal, whether they are included in the main dish or served on the side. On the following pages you will find a range of recipes for main meals, some of which include potatoes as one of the ingredients and others which are served with special potato recipes. Although there are delicious dishes for lamb, fish, chicken and beef, there are also some fabulous recipes that are suitable for vegetarians, such as Root Croustades with Sunshine (Bell) Peppers and Potato Gnocchi with Garlic & Herb Sauce. The recipes are diverse, too, influenced by many different cuisines from around the world, such as the Indian Easy Lamb & Potato Masala and Mexican Baked Tortillas. There are recipes to suit all tastes and occasions, from hearty main courses such as Irish Stew and Beef & Potato Goulash to lighter meals such as Cheese & Onion Tart and Soused Trout. Whether you are cooking for one or two, a family or a number of guests at a dinner party, you will find something here to entice you.

EASY LAMB & POTATO MASALA

It's so easy to create delicious Indian dishes at home – simply open a can of curry sauce, add a few interesting ingredients and you have a splendid dish that is sure to be popular with family or friends.

SERVES 4

INGREDIENTS:
750 g/1½ lb lean lamb (from the leg)
4 tbsp ghee or vegetable oil
500 g/1 lb potatoes, peeled and cut in large 2.5 cm/1 inch pieces
1 large onion, quartered and sliced
2 garlic cloves, crushed
175 g/6 oz mushrooms, thickly sliced
283 g/10 oz can commercial variety of tikka masala curry sauce
300 ml/½ pint/1¼ cups water
salt
3 tomatoes, halved and cut into thin slices
125g/4 oz spinach, washed and stalks trimmed
cooked rice, to serve
sprigs of fresh mint, to garnish

1 ▼ Cut the lamb into 2.5 cm/1 inch cubes. Heat the ghee or oil in a large pan, add the lamb and fry over moderate heat for 3 minutes or until sealed all over. Remove from the pan.

2 ▼ Add the potatoes, onion, garlic and mushrooms and fry for 3–4 minutes, stirring frequently. Stir the curry sauce and water into the pan, add the lamb, mix well and season with salt to taste. Cover and cook very gently for 1 hour or until the lamb is tender and cooked through, stirring occasionally.

3 ▲ Add the sliced tomatoes and the spinach to the pan, pushing the leaves well down into the mixture, then cover and cook for a further 10 minutes until the spinach is cooked and tender.

4 Serve on a bed of rice, garnished with mint sprigs.

ROSEMARY & REDCURRANT LAMB WITH LEEK & POTATO MASH

This is a pretty dish of pink tender lamb served on a light green bed of mashed leeks and potatoes.

SERVES 4

INGREDIENTS:
500 g/1 lb lean lamb fillet (tenderloin)
4 tbsp redcurrant jelly
1 tbsp chopped fresh rosemary
1 garlic clove, crushed
500 g/1 lb potatoes, diced
500 g/1 lb leeks, sliced
150 ml/¼ pint/⅔ cup fresh
  vegetable stock
4 tsp low-fat natural fromage frais
salt and pepper
freshly steamed vegetables, to serve

TO GARNISH:
chopped fresh rosemary
fresh redcurrants

1 ▼ Put the lamb in a shallow baking tin (pan). Blend 2 tablespoons of the redcurrant jelly with the rosemary, garlic and seasoning. Brush over the lamb and cook in a preheated oven at 230°C/450°F/Gas Mark 8 for 30 minutes, brushing occasionally with any cooking juices.

2 Meanwhile, place the potatoes in a saucepan and cover with water. Bring to the boil, and cook for 8 minutes until soft. Drain well. Put the leeks in a saucepan with the stock. Cover and simmer for 7–8 minutes until soft. Drain, reserving the cooking liquid.

3 ▲ Place the potato and leeks in a bowl and mash. Season to taste and stir in the fromage frais. Pile on to a warmed platter and keep warm.

4 ▼ In a saucepan, melt the remaining redcurrant jelly and stir in the leek cooking liquid. Bring the mixture to the boil for 5 minutes until reduced to a sauce.

5 Slice the lamb and arrange over the leek mash. Spoon the redcurrant sauce over the top. Garnish with chopped rosemary and redcurrants and serve immediately with freshly steamed vegetables.

SOUSED TROUT

In this recipe, fillets of trout are gently poached in a spiced vinegar, left to marinate for 24 hours and served cold with a potato salad.

SERVES 4

INGREDIENTS:
4 trout, about 250–350 g/8–12 oz each, filleted
1 onion, sliced very thinly
2 bay leaves, preferably fresh
sprigs of fresh parsley and dill, or other fresh herbs
10–12 black peppercorns
4–6 cloves
good pinch of salt
150 ml/¼ pint/⅔ cup red wine vinegar
salad leaves, to garnish

POTATO SALAD:
500 g/1 lb small new potatoes
2 tbsp French dressing
4 tbsp thick mayonnaise
3–4 spring onions (scallions), sliced

1 ▼ Trim the trout fillets, cutting off any pieces of fin. If preferred, remove the skin – use a sharp knife and, beginning at the tail end, carefully cut the flesh from the skin, pressing the knife down firmly as you go.

2 Lightly grease a shallow ovenproof dish and lay the fillets in it, packing them fairly tightly together but keeping in a single layer. Arrange the sliced onion, bay leaves and herbs over the fish.

3 ▲ Put the peppercorns, cloves, salt and vinegar into a saucepan and bring almost to the boil. Remove from the heat and pour evenly over the fish.

4 Cover with foil and cook in a preheated oven at 160°C/325°F/ Gas Mark 3 for 15 minutes. Leave until cold, and then chill thoroughly.

5 Meanwhile, make the potato salad. Cook the potatoes in boiling salted water for 10–15 minutes until just tender. Drain. While still warm, cut into large dice and place in a bowl.

6 ▼ Combine the French dressing and mayonnaise, add to the potatoes while warm and toss evenly. Leave until cold, then sprinkle with chopped spring onions (scallions).

7 Serve each portion of fish with a little of the juices, garnished with salad leaves and accompanied by the potato salad.

ROOT CROUSTADES WITH SUNSHINE (BELL) PEPPERS

This colourful combination of grated root vegetables and mixed (bell) peppers would make a stunning impression on dinner-party guests.

SERVES 4

INGREDIENTS:

1 orange (bell) pepper
1 red (bell) pepper
1 yellow (bell) pepper
3 tbsp olive oil
2 tbsp red wine vinegar
1 tsp French mustard
1 tsp clear honey
salt and pepper
sprigs of fresh flat-leaf parsley, to garnish
green vegetables, to serve

CROUSTADES:

250 g/8 oz potatoes, grated coarsely
250 g/8 oz carrots, grated coarsely
350 g/12 oz celeriac (celery root), grated coarsely
1 garlic clove, crushed
1 tbsp lemon juice
30 g/1 oz/2 tbsp butter or margarine, melted
1 egg, beaten
1 tbsp vegetable oil

1 Place the (bell) peppers on a baking sheet and bake in a preheated oven at 190°C/375°F/Gas Mark 5 for 35 minutes, turning after 20 minutes.

2 ▼ Cover with a tea towel (dish cloth) and leave to cool for 10 minutes. Peel the skin from the

cooked (bell) peppers. Cut each (bell) pepper in half and discard the core and seeds. Thinly slice the flesh into strips and place in a shallow dish.

3 Put the oil, vinegar, mustard, honey and seasoning in a small screw-top jar and shake well to mix. Pour the dressing over the (bell) pepper strips, mix well and leave to marinate for 2 hours.

4 ▲ To make the croustades, put the grated potatoes, carrots and celeriac (celery root) in a large mixing bowl and toss in the garlic and lemon juice to mix well.

5 ▼ Mix in the melted butter or margarine and the egg. Season well. Divide the mixture into 8 and pile on to 2 baking sheets lined with baking parchment, forming each into a 10 cm/4 inch round. Brush with oil.

6 Bake in a preheated oven at 220°C/425°F/Gas Mark 7 for 30–35 minutes until crisp around the edge and golden. Carefully transfer to a warmed serving dish. Heat the (bell) peppers and marinade for 2–3 minutes until warmed through. Spoon the (bell) peppers over the croustades, garnish with parsley sprigs and serve with the green vegetables.

POTATO GNOCCHI
WITH GARLIC & HERB SAUCE

These little potato dumplings are a traditional Italian appetizer, but they make a substantial meal when served with a salad and bread. If you want to serve them as an appetizer, they would serve six people.

SERVES 4

INGREDIENTS:
1 kg/2 lb old (main crop) potatoes, cut into 1 cm/½ inch pieces
60 g/2 oz/¼ cup butter or margarine
1 egg, beaten
300 g/10 oz/2 ½ cups plain (all-purpose) flour
salt

GARLIC AND HERB SAUCE:
120 ml/4 fl oz/½ cup olive oil
2 garlic cloves, chopped very finely
1 tbsp chopped fresh oregano
1 tbsp chopped fresh basil
salt and pepper

TO SERVE:
freshly grated Parmesan cheese (optional)
mixed salad
warm ciabatta

1 Cook the potatoes in boiling salted water for about 10 minutes or until tender. Drain well.

2 ▼ Press the hot potatoes through a sieve (strainer) into a large bowl. Add 1 teaspoon of salt, the butter or margarine, egg and 150 g/5 oz/1¼ cups of the flour. Mix to bind together.

3 Turn on to a lightly floured surface and knead, gradually adding the remaining flour, until a smooth, soft, slightly sticky dough is formed.

4 ▼ Flour the hands and roll the dough into 2 cm/¾ inch thick rolls. Cut into 1 cm/½ inch pieces. Press the top of each one with the floured prongs of a fork and spread out on a floured tea towel (dish cloth).

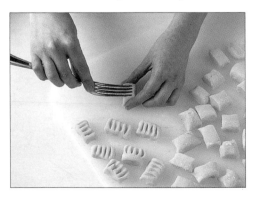

5 ▲ Bring a large saucepan of salted water to a simmer. Add the gnocchi and cook in batches for 2–3 minutes until they rise to the surface.

6 Remove with a perforated spoon and put in a warmed, greased serving dish. Cover and keep warm.

7 To make the sauce, put the oil, garlic and seasoning in a saucepan and cook gently, stirring, for 3–4 minutes until the garlic is golden. Remove from the heat and stir in the herbs. Pour over the gnocchi and serve immediately, sprinkled with Parmesan, if liked, and accompanied by salad and warm ciabatta.

POTATO PIZZA BASE

This is an unusual pizza base made from mashed potatoes and flour and it is a great way to use up any leftover boiled potatoes. Children love this base and you will soon have them asking for more.

MAKES ONE 25 CM/10 INCH ROUND

INGREDIENTS:
250 g/8 oz boiled potatoes
60 g/2 oz butter or margarine
125 g/4 oz self-raising flour
¼ tsp salt

1 ▼ If the potatoes are hot, mash them, then stir in the butter until it has melted and is distributed evenly throughout the potatoes. Leave the mashed potatoes to cool.

2 ▼ Sift the flour and salt together and stir into the mashed potato to form a soft dough.

3 If the potatoes are cold, mash them without adding the butter. Sift the flour and salt into a separate mixing bowl.

4 ▼ Cut the butter into small manageable pieces and rub in (cut in) to the mashed potatoes with your fingertips until the mixture resembles fine breadcrumbs. Stir the flour and salt mixture into the mashed potatoes to form a soft dough.

5 ▲ Either roll out or press the dough into a 25 cm/10 inch circle on a lightly greased baking sheet or pizza pan, pushing up the edge slightly to form a ridge. This base is tricky to lift before it is cooked, so you will find it easier to roll it out on the baking sheet.

6 If the base is not required for cooking immediately, cover it with clingfilm (plastic wrap) and chill it for up to 2 hours.

TOMATO SAUCE

This sauce is made with fresh tomatoes. Use the plum variety whenever available and always choose the reddest tomatoes to give a better colour and sweetness to the sauce. When plum tomatoes are readily available, make several batches of the sauce and freeze them.

MAKES ENOUGH TO COVER ONE 25 CM/10 INCH PIZZA BASE

INGREDIENTS:
1 small onion, chopped
1 small red (bell) pepper, cored, deseeded and chopped
1 garlic clove, crushed
2 tbsp olive oil
250 g/8 oz tomatoes
1 tbsp tomato purée (paste)
1 tsp soft brown sugar
2 tsp chopped fresh basil
½ tsp dried oregano
1 bay leaf
salt and pepper

1 ▼ Fry the onion, (bell) pepper and garlic gently in the oil for 5 minutes until softened but not browned.

2 ▲ Cut a cross in the base of each tomato and place in a bowl. Pour on boiling water and leave for 45 seconds. Drain, and then plunge in cold water. The skins will slide off easily.

3 ▼ Chop the tomatoes, discarding any hard cores. Add the chopped

tomatoes, tomato purée (paste), sugar, herbs and seasoning to the onion mixture. Stir well. Bring to the boil, cover and simmer gently for 30 minutes, stirring occasionally, until you have a thickish sauce.

4 ▼ Remove the bay leaf and adjust the seasoning to taste. Leave to cool completely before using.

5 This sauce will keep well in a screw-top jar in the refrigerator for up to a week.

GARDINIERE PIZZA WITH POTATO BASE

As the name implies, this colourful pizza should be topped with fresh vegetables grown in the garden, but as many of us do not have space to grow anything more than a few flowers, we have to rely on other sources. The vegetables used here are only a suggestion; you can replace them with the same quantity of any other vegetable you have available.

SERVES 2–4

INGREDIENTS:
6 fresh spinach leaves
1 Potato Base (see page 75)
1 quantity Tomato Sauce
  (see page 76)
1 tomato, sliced
1 celery stick, sliced thinly
½ green (bell) pepper, sliced thinly
1 baby courgette (zucchini), sliced
30 g/1 oz asparagus tips
30 g/1 oz sweetcorn, defrosted
  if frozen
30 g/1 oz peas, defrosted if frozen
4 spring onions (scallions), trimmed
  and chopped
1 tbsp chopped fresh mixed herbs, such
  as tarragon and parsley
60 g/2 oz Mozzarella cheese, grated
2 tbsp grated fresh Parmesan cheese
1 artichoke heart
olive oil, for drizzling
salt and pepper

2 ▼ Roll out or press the potato base, using a rolling pin or your hands, into a large 25 cm/10 inch circle on a large greased baking sheet or pizza pan and push up the edge a little to form a rim. Spread with the Tomato Sauce.

4 ▼ Mix together the Mozzarella and Parmesan cheeses in a separate bowl, then sprinkle over the pizza. Place the artichoke heart in the centre. Drizzle the pizza with a little olive oil and season well.

1 ▼ Remove any stalks from the spinach and wash the leaves in plenty of cold water. Pat dry with paper towels.

3 ▼ Arrange the spinach on the sauce, followed by the tomatos. Top with the remaining vegetables and herbs.

5 Bake in a preheated oven at 200°C/400°F/Gas Mark 6 for 18–20 minutes, or until the edges are crisp and golden. Serve immediately.

MEXICAN BAKED TORTILLAS WITH TOMATO SALSA

Soft flour tortillas are filled with potatoes, (bell) peppers and refried beans. If refried beans are not available, substitute red kidney beans.

SERVES 4

INGREDIENTS:

3 tbsp vegetable oil
1 onion, chopped
1–2 garlic cloves, crushed
¼ green (bell) pepper, cored, deseeded and chopped
¼ red (bell) pepper, cored, deseeded and chopped
350 g/12 oz cooked potato, diced
¼ large fresh green chilli, deseeded and finely chopped
1 tbsp chopped coriander (cilantro)
200 g/7 oz can refried beans
salt and pepper
4 soft flour tortillas
125g/4 oz Cheddar cheese, grated
sprigs of fresh coriander (cilantro), to garnish

TOMATO SALSA:

150 ml/¼ pint/⅔ cup tomato juice
4 tomatoes, finely chopped
5 cm/2 inch piece cucumber, finely chopped
1 small onion, finely chopped
1 tbsp chopped fresh coriander (cilantro)

1 ▼ Heat the oil in a large frying pan (skillet) and gently fry the onion and garlic until softened. Add the (bell) peppers, potatoes and chilli and cook for 3–4 minutes more, until browned.

2 ▼ Add the coriander (cilantro) and refried beans to the frying pan (skillet) and mix well. Stir until thoroughly heated. Season with salt and pepper.

3 Lay the tortillas on a work surface (counter) and divide the filling equally between them. Roll up and place in a greased baking dish, folded sides up. Scatter the grated cheese on top and bake in a preheated oven at 180°C/350°F/Gas Mark 4 for 20–25 minutes.

4 ▼ Meanwhile mix all the salsa ingredients together in a small mixing bowl, seasoning well. Chill until ready to serve.

5 Garnish the baked tortillas with sprigs of fresh coriander (cilantro) and serve hot, accompanied by the salsa.

CHEESE & ONION TART

This tart is made with a potato 'pastry' case, which is filled with a tasty cheese and onion mixture. To add a stronger flavour of cheese, add 2 tablespoons of grated Parmesan to the filling mixture.

SERVES 6

INGREDIENTS:
2 large onions, chopped
175 g/6 oz Cheddar cheese, grated
3 eggs, beaten
salt and pepper
1 tbsp chopped fresh parsley or chives

POTATO PASTRY:
750 g/1½ lb old (main crop) potatoes,
  peeled
15 g/½ oz/1 tbsp butter
60 g/2 oz/½ cup plain (all-purpose)
  flour
1 egg, beaten
salt and pepper

1 Prepare the pastry. Put the potatoes in a saucepan of lightly salted boiling water and boil for 20 minutes until tender. Drain well and mash until no lumps remain.

2 ▼ Mix the butter, flour and egg into the mashed potato. Season well with salt and pepper.

3 ▼ Turn the potato pastry into a 25 cm/10 inch flan dish (quiche pan). Using floured hands, press the pastry over the base and up the sides. Prick the base all over with a fork. Line with foil and bake in a preheated oven at 200°C/400°F/Gas Mark 6 for 15 minutes.

4 Meanwhile, cook the onions in a small amount of boiling water for about 10 minutes until just tender. Drain the onions well and return to the pan.

5 ▲ Mix the grated cheese into the onions and stir to melt. Cool slightly, then stir in the beaten eggs. Season well and add the parsley or chives.

6 Remove the tart case from the oven and take out the foil. Leave to cool for 10 minutes. Reduce the temperature to 190°C/375°F/Gas Mark 5.

7 Pour the cheesy onion mixture into the tart case. Return to the oven and bake for 25–30 minutes until set and golden brown.

BEEF & POTATO GOULASH

Potatoes are the most natural accompaniment to goulash, and in this recipe they are actually cooked in the goulash! For a change, you may prefer to substitute small, scrubbed new potatoes for the ordinary potatoes in this recipe.

SERVES 4

INGREDIENTS:

2 tablespoons vegetable oil
1 large onion, sliced
2 garlic cloves, crushed
750 g/1½ lb stewing steak, cut into chunks
2 tbsp paprika
425 g/14 oz can chopped tomatoes
2 tbsp tomato purée (paste)
1 large red (bell) pepper, cored, deseeded and chopped
175 g/6 oz mushrooms, wiped and sliced
600 ml/1 pint/2½ cups beef stock
500 g/1 lb potatoes, peeled and cut into large chunks
1 tbsp cornflour (cornstarch)
salt and pepper

TO GARNISH:

4 tbsp crème fraîche or natural yogurt
paprika
chopped fresh parsley

1 ▼ Heat the oil in a large saucepan and gently fry the onion and garlic for 3–4 minutes until softened. Add the chunks of steak and cook over a high heat for about 3 minutes until browned all over.

2 ▼ Add the paprika and stir well. Add the tomatoes, tomato purée (paste), red (bell) pepper and mushrooms. Cook for 2 minutes, stirring constantly.

3 Pour in the stock. Bring to the boil, then reduce the heat. Cover and simmer for about 1½ hours until the meat is tender.

4 Add the potatoes and cook, covered, for a further 20–30 minutes until tender.

5 ▲ Blend the cornflour (cornstarch) with a little water and add to the saucepan, stirring until thickened and blended. Cook for 1 minute, then season with salt and pepper. Top with crème fraîche or natural yogurt, sprinkle over the paprika and chopped fresh parsley and serve.

SPANISH CHICKEN CASSEROLE

Tomatoes, olives, peppers and potatoes, with a splash of Spanish red wine, make this marvellous peasant-style dish. The olives mellow during cooking to give a delicious subtle flavour.

SERVES 4

INGREDIENTS:

30 g/1 oz/¼ cup plain (all-purpose) flour
1 tsp salt
pepper
1 tbsp paprika
4 chicken portions
3 tbsp olive oil
1 large onion, chopped
2 garlic cloves, crushed
6 tomatoes, chopped, or 425 g/14 oz
    can chopped tomatoes
1 green (bell) pepper, cored, deseeded
    and chopped
150 ml/¼ pint/⅔ cup Spanish red wine
300 ml/½ pint/1¼ cups chicken stock
3 medium potatoes, peeled and
    quartered
12 pitted black olives
1 bay leaf
crusty bread, to serve

1 Put the flour, salt, pepper and paprika into a large polythene bag. Rinse the chicken portions, put them into the bag and shake to coat in the seasoned flour.

2 ▼ Heat the oil in a large flameproof casserole dish. Add the chicken portions and cook over a

medium–high heat for 5–8 minutes until well-browned on each side. Lift out of the casserole with a perforated spoon and set aside.

3 ▼ Add the onion and garlic to the casserole and cook for a few minutes until browned. Add the tomatoes and (bell) pepper and cook for a further 2–3 minutes.

4 ▼ Return the chicken to the casserole. Add the wine, stock and potatoes, and then the olives and bay leaf. Cover and bake in a preheated oven at 190°C/375°F/Gas Mark 5 for 1 hour until the chicken is tender.

5 Check the seasoning, adding more salt and pepper if necessary. Serve hot with chunks of crusty bread.

IRISH STEW WITH PARSLEY DUMPLINGS

This traditional recipe makes a hearty stew with fluffy parsley dumplings, but you can make it without the dumplings and serve it with crusty bread instead. Cubes of lean lamb shoulder could be used in place of the cutlets.

SERVES 4

INGREDIENTS:
2 tbsp vegetable oil
2 large onions, sliced
1 leek, sliced
1 large carrot, sliced
2 celery sticks, sliced
900 ml/1½ pints/3¾ cups lamb stock
750 g/1½ lb lean lamb cutlets, trimmed
60 g/2 oz/¼ cup pearl barley
2 large potatoes, peeled and cut into large chunks
salt and pepper
chopped fresh parsley, to garnish

DUMPLINGS:
90 g/3 oz self-raising flour
30 g/1 oz/¼ cup porridge oats
2 tbsp chopped fresh parsley
pinch of salt
60 g/2 oz suet
chilled water, to mix

1 ▼ First make the dumplings. Put the flour, oats, parsley and salt into a large mixing bowl. Stir in the suet. Add sufficient chilled water to make a soft, but not sticky, dough. Shape into 8 dumplings, cover with a tea towel (dish cloth) and set aside.

2 ▼ Heat the vegetable oil in a large saucepan and gently fry the onions, leek, carrot and celery for 5 minutes, without browning.

3 Add the stock, lamb and pearl barley to the saucepan. Bring to the boil and then reduce the heat. Cover and simmer for 30–40 minutes, adding the potatoes after 20 minutes.

4 ▲ Add the dumplings to the saucepan. Cover and simmer for 15–20 minutes until the dumplings are light and fluffy.

5 Season the stew with salt and pepper, garnish with parsley and serve immediately while still hot.

PIES & BAKES

One of the best ways to use potatoes is in fish and meat pies and vegetable bakes that are cooked in the oven. In this chapter you will find a wide selection of traditional pies, such as Shepherd's Pie, Mariner's Pie and Moussaka, along with unique variations, such as Sea Bream & Sweet Potato Pie. There are also several hotpot dishes, which are cooked in a casserole and make wonderful one-pot meals. Usually topped with mashed potato or potato slices, most of the recipes on the following pages make hearty dishes that are ideal for autumn or winter meals. However, there are a few less robust dishes, such as Spring Chicken & Potato Bake, which uses lots of herbs and garden vegetables, and Layered Root Vegetable Gratin, which can be served either as a vegetarian main course with some crusty bread or as a side dish to a meat-based meal. Many of the recipes are adaptable, and you may like to substitute your favourite vegetables for the ones suggested in the recipe, or vary them according to seasonal availability.

MARINER'S PIE (PAGE 85)

OCEAN PIE

This tasty fish pie combines a mixture of fish and shellfish. You can use a wide variety of fish – whatever is easily available.

SERVES 4

INGREDIENTS:
500 g/1 lb cod or haddock fillet, skinned
250 g/8 oz salmon steak
450 ml/¾ pint/scant 2 cups milk
1 bay leaf
1 kg/2 lb potatoes, peeled
60 g/2 oz/⅓ cup peeled prawns (shrimp), thawed if frozen
60 g/2 oz/¼ cup butter or margarine
30 g/1 oz/4 tbsp plain (all-purpose) flour
2–4 tbsp white wine
1 tsp chopped fresh dill, or ½ tsp dried dill
2 tbsp drained capers
salt and pepper
few whole prawns (shrimp) in their shells, to garnish

1 ▼ Put the cod or haddock and salmon into a saucepan with 300 ml/ ½ pint/1¼ cups of the milk, the bay leaf and seasoning. Bring to the boil, cover and simmer gently for 10–15 minutes until tender.

2 Meanwhile, coarsely chop the potatoes and cook in boiling salted water until tender.

3 ▼ Drain the fish, reserving 300 ml/ ½ pint/1¼ cups of the cooking liquid (make up with more milk if necessary). Flake the fish, discarding any bones, and place in a shallow ovenproof dish. Add the prawns (shrimp).

4 Melt half the butter or margarine in a saucepan, add the flour and cook, stirring, for a minute or so. Gradually stir in the reserved stock and the wine and bring to the boil. Add the herbs, capers and seasoning to taste and simmer until thickened. Pour over the fish and mix well.

5 Drain the potatoes and mash them, adding the remaining butter or margarine, seasoning and sufficient milk to give the potatoes a piping consistency.

6 ▲ Put the mashed potato into a piping bag fitted with a large star nozzle (tip) and pipe whirls over the fish to cover completely.

7 Cook in a preheated oven at 200°C/400°F/Gas Mark 6 for about 25 minutes until piping hot and browned. Serve garnished with whole prawns (shrimp).

MARINER'S PIE

Make this cheap and cheerful fish pie with coley or any other inexpensive white fish.

SERVES 4

INGREDIENTS:
750 g/1½ lb potatoes
2 large leeks, sliced
300 ml/½ pint/1¼ cups plus 2 tbsp milk
1 tbsp chopped fresh parsley
60 g/2 oz/¼ cup butter
60 g/2 oz/½ cup plain (all-purpose) flour
750 g/1½ lb skinned and boned coley, cut into chunks
1 egg
salt and pepper
chopped fresh parsley, to garnish

TO SERVE:
French (green) beans
tomatoes

1 Boil the potatoes in lightly salted water for about 15 minutes until tender. Meanwhile, cook the leeks in lightly salted boiling water for about 8 minutes.

2 ▼ Drain the potatoes and leeks, reserving the cooking liquid. Mash the potatoes with 2 tbsp of the milk and half the butter. Make the remaining milk up to 600 ml/1 pint/2½ cups with the cooking liquid from the potatoes and leeks. Add the parsley to the milk mixture.

3 ▼ Melt the remaining butter in a saucepan. Add the flour and cook gently, stirring, for 1 minute. Gradually stir in the milk and parsley mixture. Heat, stirring constantly, until thickened and smooth. Season to taste.

4 Grease a large, shallow ovenproof dish. Put the fish in the dish and arrange the cooked leeks on top.

5 ▼ Pour the parsley sauce over the fish and leeks.

6 Pipe or spoon the potatoes on top, covering completely. Bake in a preheated oven at 190°C/375°F/ Gas Mark 5 for 25–30 minutes until the potatoes are golden.

7 Garnish the pie with parsley and serve with the beans and tomatoes.

SEA BREAM & SWEET POTATO PIE

This is a fish pie with a difference – a creamy fish sauce topped with golden sweet potatoes for a substantial supper-time meal.

SERVES 6

INGREDIENTS:

15 g/⅓ oz/1 tbsp butter
3 tbsp groundnut oil
250 g/8 oz sweet potatoes, unpeeled and sliced thinly
1 onion, chopped finely
750 g/1½ lb sea bream fillets, skinned and cut into large pieces
2 hard-boiled (hard-cooked) eggs, chopped
sprigs of fresh parsley, to garnish

CURRY SAUCE:

45 g/1½ oz/3 tbsp butter
2 tbsp plain (all-purpose) flour
300 ml/½ pint/1¼ cups milk
90 g/3 oz/¾ cup mature (sharp) Cheddar cheese, grated
1 tsp curry powder
2 tbsp chopped fresh flat-leaf parsley
salt and pepper

1 ▼ In a large frying pan (skillet), melt the butter with 2 tablespoons of the oil. Fry the sweet potatoes in batches for 1–2 minutes on each side, without allowing to soften. Remove with a perforated spoon and drain on paper towels.

2 ▼ Add the onion to the pan and fry for 5 minutes. Add the sea bream and cook for a further 5 minutes. Remove the pan from the heat and stir in the eggs. Transfer the fish mixture to an ovenproof dish.

3 To make the sauce, melt the butter in a saucepan, add the flour and stir over a low heat for 1–2 minutes. Remove from the heat and gradually stir in the milk. Return to the heat and stir for a further 2–3 minutes. Add two-thirds of the cheese, the curry powder, parsley and seasoning.

4 ▼ Pour the sauce over the fish and mix gently. Layer the sweet potato over the top, overlapping the slices. Brush with the remaining oil and sprinkle with the remaining cheese. Bake in a preheated oven at 180°C/350°F/Gas Mark 4 for 30 minutes until golden. Garnish with parsley and serve.

SHEPHERD'S PIE

Minced (ground) lamb or beef is cooked with onions, carrots, herbs and tomatoes and topped with piped creamed potatoes to make a hearty and nourishing dish.

SERVES 4–5

INGREDIENTS:

750 g/1½ lb lean minced (ground) lamb
   or beef
2 onions, chopped
250 g/8 oz carrots, diced
1–2 garlic cloves, crushed
1 tbsp plain (all-purpose) flour
200 ml/7 fl oz/scant 1 cup beef stock
200 g/7 oz can chopped tomatoes
1 tsp Worcestershire sauce
1 tsp chopped fresh sage or oregano, or
   ½ tsp dried sage or oregano
750 g–1 kg/1½–2 lb potatoes
30 g/1 oz/2 tbsp butter or margarine
3–4 tbsp milk
125 g/4 oz button mushrooms, sliced
   (optional)
salt and pepper

1 Place the meat in a heavy-based saucepan with no extra fat and cook gently, stirring frequently, until the meat begins to brown.

2 ▼ Add the onions, carrots and garlic and continue to cook gently for about 10 minutes. Stir in the flour and cook for a minute or so, then gradually stir in the stock and tomatoes and bring to the boil.

3 ▼ Add the Worcestershire sauce, seasoning and herbs, cover the pan and simmer gently for about 25 minutes, giving an occasional stir.

4 Cook the potatoes in boiling salted water until tender, then drain thoroughly and mash, beating in the butter or margarine, seasoning and sufficient milk to give a piping consistency. Place in a piping bag fitted with a large star nozzle (tip).

5 ▼ Stir the mushrooms, if using, into the meat and adjust the seasoning. Turn the mixture into a shallow ovenproof dish.

6 Pipe the potatoes evenly all over the meat. Cook in a preheated oven at 200°C/400°F/Gas Mark 6 for about 30 minutes until piping hot and the potatoes are golden brown.

SARDINE & POTATO BAKE

Fresh sardines bear very little resemblance to the canned varieties. They are now readily available, frozen and sometimes fresh, so this traditional dish from Liguria can now be enjoyed by all.

SERVES 4

INGREDIENTS:

1 kg/2 lb potatoes, peeled
1 kg/2 lb sardines, defrosted if frozen
1 tbsp olive oil, plus extra for oiling
1 onion, peeled and chopped
2–3 garlic cloves, crushed
2 tbsp freshly chopped parsley
350 g/12 oz ripe tomatoes, peeled and sliced, or 425 g/15 oz can peeled tomatoes, partly drained and chopped
1–2 tbsp freshly chopped Italian herbs, such as oregano, thyme, rosemary and marjoram
150 ml/¼ pint/⅔ cup dry white wine
salt and pepper

1 Put the potatoes in a saucepan of salted water, bring to the boil, cover and simmer for 10 minutes. Drain well and leave to cool. When cool enough to handle, cut into slices about 5 mm/¼ inch thick.

2 ▲ Gut and clean the sardines. Cut off their heads and tails and then slit open the length of the belly. Turn the fish over so the skin is upwards and press firmly along the backbone to loosen the bones. Turn over again and carefully remove the backbone. Wash the fish in cold water, drain well and dry them on paper towels.

3 Heat the oil in a frying pan (skillet) and fry the onion and garlic until soft, but not coloured.

4 ▼ Arrange the potatoes in a well-oiled ovenproof dish and sprinkle with the onions. Scatter over the parsley and add plenty of seasoning.

5 ▼ Lay the open sardines over the potatoes, skin-side down, then cover with the tomatoes and the rest of the herbs. Pour on the wine and season.

6 Cook, uncovered, in a preheated oven at 190°C/375°F/Gas Mark 5 for about 40 minutes until the fish is tender. If the casserole seems to be drying out, add another couple of tablespoons of wine.

LAYERED ROOT VEGETABLE GRATIN

The word 'gratin' usually describes a baked crust made from eggs and flour. In this recipe an assortment of vegetables are cooked in a light nutmeg sauce with a potato and cheese topping. The gratin makes a great vegetarian main course, but can also be served as an accompaniment.

SERVES 6

INGREDIENTS:
250 g/8 oz/2 large carrots
250 g/8 oz baby parsnips
1 fennel bulb
500 g/1 lb/3 potatoes
90 g/3 oz/⅜ cup low-fat spread
30 g/1 oz/¼ cup plain (all-purpose) flour
300 ml/½ pint/1¼ cups skimmed milk
½ tsp ground nutmeg
1 egg, beaten
30 g/1 oz/¼ cup freshly grated Parmesan cheese
salt and pepper

TO SERVE:
crusty bread
mixed salad

1 ▼ Cut the carrots and parsnips into thin lengthways strips. Cook in boiling water for 5 minutes. Drain well and transfer to an ovenproof baking dish.

2 Thinly slice the fennel and cook in boiling water for 2–3 minutes. Drain well and add to the carrots and parsnips. Season.

3 ▲ Peel and dice the potatoes into 2 cm/¾ inch cubes. Cook in boiling water for 6 minutes. Drain well and set aside.

4 Gently melt half the low-fat spread in a saucepan and stir in the flour. Remove from the heat and gradually mix in the milk. Return to the heat and stir until thickened. Season and stir in the nutmeg. Leave to cool for 10 minutes.

5 ▼ Beat in the egg and spoon the mixture over the vegetables. Arrange the potatoes on top and sprinkle over the grated cheese. Dot with the remaining low-fat spread.

6 Bake in a preheated oven at 180°C/350°F/Gas Mark 4 for 1 hour until the vegetables are tender.

7 Serve hot with crusty bread and a mixed salad.

SCALLOPED POTATO PIE

Layers of sliced potatoes with onions and diced bacon are topped with crispy browned cheese. This dish can be cooked with stock for everyday meals or with cream if you want to make it more special.

SERVES 4

INGREDIENTS:

1.25 kg/2½ lb potatoes
2 large onions, chopped finely
2 garlic cloves, crushed (optional)
175–250 g/6–8 oz lean bacon, derinded and diced
2 tbsp chopped fresh dill, or ¼ tsp dried dill
450 ml/¾ pint/scant 2 cups stock, milk or single (light) cream
15 g/½ oz/1 tbsp butter or margarine, melted
60 g/2 oz/½ cup mature (sharp) Cheddar, Gouda (Dutch) or Emmenthal (Swiss) cheese, grated
salt and pepper

1 Slice the potatoes, either by hand or using a food processor.

2 ▲ Thoroughly grease a large ovenproof dish or roasting tin (pan). Arrange a layer of sliced potatoes in the dish or tin (pan) and sprinkle with half the onions. Season lightly.

3 ▼ Add a second layer of potatoes, then the rest of the onions, the garlic, if using, the bacon, dill and seasoning, sprinkling evenly. Add a final layer of potatoes, arranging them in an attractive pattern.

4 Gently heat the stock, milk or cream and pour over the potatoes. Brush the top layer of potatoes with the melted butter or margarine and cover with greased foil or a lid.

5 Bake the potatoes in a preheated oven at 200°C/400°F/Gas Mark 6 for about 1 hour.

6 ▼ Remove the foil or lid and sprinkle the cheese over the potatoes.

7 Return the dish, uncovered, to the oven for a further 30–45 minutes until the cheese is well browned on top and the potatoes are tender. Serve immediately while still hot.

SAVOURY HOTPOT

This hearty lamb stew is full of vegetables and herbs and topped with a layer of crisp, golden potato slices.

SERVES 4

INGREDIENTS:
8 middle neck lamb chops, neck of lamb or any stewing lamb on the bone
1–2 garlic cloves, crushed
2 lamb's kidneys (optional)
1 large onion, sliced thinly
1 leek, sliced
2–3 carrots, sliced
1 tsp chopped fresh tarragon or sage, or ½ tsp dried tarragon or sage
1 kg/2 lb potatoes, sliced thinly
300 ml/½ pint/1¼ cups stock
30 g/1 oz/2 tbsp butter or margarine, melted, or 1 tbsp vegetable oil
salt and pepper
chopped fresh parsley, to garnish

1 ▼ Trim the lamb of any excess fat, season well with salt and pepper and arrange in a large ovenproof casserole. Sprinkle with the garlic.

2 If using kidneys, remove the skin, halve the kidneys and cut out the cores. Chop into small pieces and sprinkle over the lamb.

3 ▲ Place the onion, leek and carrots over the lamb, allowing the pieces to slip in between the meat, then sprinkle with the herbs.

4 Arrange the potato slices evenly and overlapping over the contents of the casserole.

5 Bring the stock to the boil, season with salt and pepper, then pour over the casserole.

6 ▼ Brush the potatoes with melted butter or margarine, or oil, cover with greased foil or a lid and cook in a preheated oven at 180°C/350°F/ Gas Mark 4 for 1½ hours.

7 Remove the foil or lid from the potatoes, increase the oven temperature to 220°C/425°F/ Gas Mark 7 and return the casserole to the oven for about 30 minutes until the potatoes are browned. Garnish with chopped parsley and serve.

BACON, ONION & POTATO HOTPOT

Simple, straightforward and satisfying, this homely casserole is perfect for chilly winter days.

SERVES 4

INGREDIENTS:
60 g/2 oz/¼ cup butter or margarine
1 kg/2 lb old (main crop) potatoes, sliced
500 g/1 lb onions, sliced
900 ml/1½ pints/3½ cups chicken stock
500 g/1 lb streaky bacon
salt and pepper
steamed broccoli, to serve

1 ▼ Grease a 2 litre/3½ pint/2 quart casserole with some of the butter or margarine. Layer the potatoes and onions alternately in the casserole dish, seasoning each layer. Finish with a layer of potatoes.

2 ▼ Pour the stock over the potatoes and dot the surface with the remaining butter or margarine. Cover and bake in a preheated oven at 190°C/ 375°F/Gas Mark 5 for 45 minutes.

3 ▼ Remove the lid from the casserole and return to the oven for a further 30 minutes until the potatoes are golden brown.

4 Meanwhile, cook the bacon under a preheated moderate grill (broiler) until cooked, but not too crisp.

5 ▲ Put the bacon on top of the potatoes and cook in the oven for a further 10 minutes. Serve at once on warmed plates, with broccoli.

LAMB & POTATO MOUSSAKA

Minced (ground) lamb makes a very tasty and authentic moussaka. For a change, use minced (ground) beef.

SERVES 4

INGREDIENTS:
1 large aubergine (eggplant), sliced
1 tbsp olive or vegetable oil
1 onion, chopped finely
1 garlic clove, crushed
350 g/12 oz minced (ground) lamb
250 g/8 oz mushrooms, sliced
425 g/14 oz can chopped tomatoes with herbs
150 ml/¼ pint/⅔ cup lamb or vegetable stock
2 tbsp cornflour (cornstarch)
2 tbsp water
500 g/1 lb potatoes, parboiled for 10 minutes and sliced
2 eggs
125 g/4 oz/½ cup low-fat soft cheese
150 ml/¼ pint/⅔ cup natural yogurt
60 g/2 oz/½ cup grated mature (sharp) Cheddar cheese
salt and pepper
fresh flat-leaf parsley, to garnish
green salad, to serve

1 ▼ Lay the aubergine (eggplant) slices on a clean surface and sprinkle liberally with salt, to extract the bitter juices. Leave for 10 minutes then turn the slices over and repeat. Put in a colander, rinse and drain well.

2 ▲ Meanwhile, heat the oil in a saucepan and fry the onion and garlic for 3–4 minutes. Add the lamb and mushrooms and cook for 5 minutes, until browned. Stir in the tomatoes and stock, bring to the boil and simmer for 10 minutes. Mix the cornflour (cornstarch) with the water and stir into the pan. Cook, stirring, until thickened.

3 Spoon half the mixture into an ovenproof dish. Cover with the aubergine (eggplant) slices, then the remaining lamb mixture. Arrange the sliced potatoes on top.

4 ▼ Beat together the eggs, soft cheese, yogurt and seasoning. Pour over the potatoes to cover them completely. Sprinkle with the grated cheese.

5 Bake in a preheated oven at 190°C/375°F/Gas Mark 5 for 45 minutes until the topping is set and golden brown. Garnish with flat-leaf parsley and serve with a green salad.

SPRING CHICKEN & POTATO BAKE

Make this delicious dish when new potatoes are in season. A medium onion or a few shallots can be substituted for the spring onions (scallions) in the recipe.

SERVES 4

INGREDIENTS:
2 tbsp olive oil
4 chicken breasts
1 bunch spring onions (scallions), trimmed and chopped
350 g/12 oz young spring carrots, scrubbed and sliced
125 g/4 oz dwarf green beans, trimmed and sliced
600 ml/1 pint/2¼ cups chicken stock
350 g/12 oz small new potatoes, scrubbed
1 small bunch mixed fresh herbs, such as thyme, rosemary, bay and parsley
salt and pepper
2 tbsp cornflour (cornstarch)
2–3 tbsp cold water
sprigs of fresh mixed herbs, to garnish

1 Heat the oil in a large flameproof casserole and add the chicken breasts. Gently fry for 5–8 minutes until browned on both sides. Lift from the casserole with a perforated spoon and set aside.

2 ▲ Add the spring onions (scallions), carrots and green beans and gently fry for 3–4 minutes.

3 ▼ Return the chicken breasts to the casserole and pour in the chicken stock. Add the potatoes and herbs. Season with salt and pepper. Bring to the boil, then cover the casserole and transfer to the oven. Bake in a preheated oven at 190°C/375°F/ Gas Mark 5 for 40–50 minutes until the potatoes are tender.

4 ▲ Blend the cornflour (cornstarch) with the cold water. Add to the casserole, stirring until blended and thickened. Cover and cook for a further 5 minutes. Garnish with fresh herbs and serve.

BEEF PIE WITH RED CABBAGE

This stew of slow-cooked braising steak with onions and potatoes is topped with a shortcrust pastry and served with pickled red cabbage. A deep casserole dish works best for this pie.

SERVES 4

INGREDIENTS:
2 tbsp vegetable oil
750 g/1½ lb braising steak, trimmed
    and cubed
900 ml/1½ pints/3¾ cups beef stock
2 medium onions, chopped
1 kg/2 lb potatoes, peeled and cubed
salt and pepper
pickled red cabbage, to serve

PASTRY:
250 g/8 oz/2 cups plain (all-purpose)
    flour
¼ tsp salt
100 g/4 oz/½ cup margarine
6-7 tbsp chilled water
milk, for brushing

1 ▼ Heat the vegetable oil in a large saucepan. Add the beef and fry over a high heat for 5–8 minutes until browned on all sides. Add the stock. Bring to the boil, then cover and reduce the heat. Simmer for 1½ hours until the meat is tender.

2 Add the onions and potatoes. Bring back to the boil, then reduce the heat and simmer, uncovered, for about 20 minutes until the potatoes are tender. Season to taste.

3 Transfer the meat and potato mixture to a 2 litre/3 pint/2 quart casserole dish and leave to cool slightly.

4 ▼ Meanwhile make the pastry. Sift the flour and salt into a bowl. Cut the margarine into pieces and add to the bowl. Rub in (cut in) until the mixture resembles fine breadcrumbs. Add sufficient chilled water to make a soft, but not sticky, dough. Knead the dough lightly for a few seconds until it is smooth.

5 ▼ Roll out the pastry on a lightly floured work surface (counter) to fit the top of the casserole. Make a small hole in the middle so steam can escape.

6 Lift the pastry on to the top of the casserole and pinch the edges to seal, trimming off any extra. Brush with a little milk. Stand on a baking sheet and bake in a preheated oven at 200°C/400°F/Gas Mark 6 for 25–30 minutes until the pastry is cooked and golden. Serve with the pickled red cabbage.

INDEX